CLEMATIS

CLEMATIS
Barry Fretwell

COLLINS

Frontispiece: 'Lady Betty Balfour'

Text and illustrations © Barry Fretwell 1989

First published in 1989 by
William Collins Sons & Co Ltd
London · Glasgow · Sydney
Auckland · Toronto · Johannesburg

British Library Cataloguing in Publication Data
Fretwell, Barry
Clematis
1.   Gardens. Clematis
I.   Title
635.9'33111

ISBN 0-00-411335-7

Produced by the Justin Knowles Publishing Group
9 Colleton Crescent, Exeter, Devon EX2 4BY

Designer: Michael Head

Typeset by August Filmsetting, Haydock, St. Helens
Printed and bound in Portugal

CONTENTS

INTRODUCTION

The past decade has seen a revival in the popularity of clematis that was theirs during the latter part of the 19th and the beginning of the 20th century. Until recently, visitors to major exhibitions, such as London's Chelsea Flower Show, would have seen displays comprised mainly of mid-season, large-flowered clematis hybrids with a few early-season species. And yet there is a wealth of delight and variety of form and colour to be found in the later flowering species. They are now exhibited at flower shows staged in August or September up and down the country.

The aim of this book is to extend the knowledge of the available range of these diverse and lovely plants and to suggest their multiple uses, from the combination of one clematis with another to interplanting among other plants. Those chiefly familiar with the better known large-flowered hybrids will be amazed at the vast choice that exists and will be intrigued by the beauty of the species; for the clematis enthusiasts, perhaps already growing the species, along with their larger sisters, there is new knowledge to be gained about recently available or even newly discovered species. Catalogues that have remained more or less unchanged for many years are extending their range due partly to new introductions of species mainly from China and the Antipodes, and partly to the breeding of new cultivars.

The word 'clematis' is derived from the Greek 'klema' which described an obscure kind of vine or climbing plant. There is only one correct way to pronounce 'clematis' – that is, with the accent on the first syllable and a short 'a'. Clematis belong to the order of *Ranunculaceae,* which may initially seem surprising, but the family likeness can be seen in the flower shape of buttercup, anemone and aquilegia; however, unlike these plants, clematis have no true petals. They have been replaced by the sepals, those parts that, on most flowering plants, enclose the petals and that insignificantly fold back to the stem as the flower grows and expands. The sepals of clematis are unsurpassed in their large size and beautiful colouring; they are usually four in number, although there can be as many as eight.

There are well over 250 species, which are widely distributed over the temperate and tropical regions of the world. They occur, however, mostly in the northern hemisphere – several species are native to Europe – and it is the clematis from the cooler regions that are of primary interest in the following pages. The acquisition of less well-known clematis, many of which are illustrated, requires a visit to a specialist nursery. Some of the plants offered will be unusual and even rare, the difficulty of propagation being reflected in the slightly higher price asked for them. With this, however, should go the assurance of obtaining a plant that is true to name.

The photographs in this book, although limited to approximately one-third of the clematis in cultivation, are designed to show, in some measure, the diversity of this large family. A main feature of clematis is the stunning effect of multiple flowers but, for ease of identification, most of the photographs portray even the small-flowering varieties and species as a single flower or as a small group. Careful note should be taken, therefore, of the size of flower given in the text.

Barry Fretwell

THE HISTORY OF CLEMATIS

Little is known about the first introduction of clematis in the 16th century, and the initial breeding of them remains obscure. In comparison with some other garden plants, roses, pinks and tulips, for example, the hybrid clematis is a relative newcomer. Apart from Britain's only native species, *C. vitalba* (old man's beard, see page 143), the only climbing clematis grown until the 18th century were *C. viticella*, *C. flammula* (see page 105) and *C. cirrhosa* (see page 97), which were introduced to Britain from southern Europe at the end of the 16th century; although the purple *C. viticella* (see page 144) had produced sports of double form and different colours. None of the 18th-century introductions from America, such as *C. viorna* (see page 142) and *C. crispa* (see page 100), although garden-worthy plants in their own right, made any contribution to hybridizing. The first hybrid between two clematis species is accepted as being *C. × eriostemon* 'Hendersonii' (see page 104), which was raised in 1835 by a Mr Henderson at the old Pineapple Nursery, St John's Wood in London, as a cross between *C. viticella* (see page 144) and *C. integrifolia* (see page 112). The same cross was achieved later, in 1857, at the French nursery of Bonamy Frères in Toulouse, the resulting hybrid being similar, with blue-purple flowers. (I did a repeat of this cross in 1981, the offspring being of a more rosy-purple colouring with yellow stamens). It was the acquisition of *C. patens* (introduced from Japan by Siebold about 1836), *C. lanuginosa* (discovered in China in 1850 and brought back by Robert Fortune) and *C. florida* (the manner of whose introduction from China remains unknown and their subsequent crossing with *C. viticella* that gave rise to the modern large-flowered hybrids.

During the period from 1860 to 1890 more new varieties were raised than at any time in the history of clematis; catalogues of the time list as many as 200 large-flowered hybrids, and a good number of those are still among the finest available today. Many worthwhile hybrids raised in the late 19th century were discarded, simply because they did not reach the large flower size that was the criterion of the day. This is a sad loss, as they would have been valued today given the greater sophistication in gardening taste. It was fashionable at that time to name new varieties after members of the royal family and the aristocracy, the personages so perpetuated being in many cases the patrons of the nurserymen who raised the new plants.

In Britain some of the leading clematis hybridizers of the 1860s included Cripps & Son of Tunbridge Wells, Kent, C. Noble of Sunningdale, Berkshire, Isaac Anderson-Henry of Edinburgh and, of course, George Jackman & Sons of Woking, Surrey. They have left us legacies of their work that still rank among the finest after more than one century. When, in 1862, Jackman first flowered *C. × jackmanii* (probably the most widely known clematis ever

W.G.S.

Clematis lanuginosa

raised) the parentage was given as *C. lanuginosa* pollinated by *C. viticella* 'Atrorubens' and *C. × eriostemon* 'Hendersonii'. For the past hundred years every single book on clematis has given this same information without ever questioning its validity. However, because the stigma has been dusted with the pollen of six different plants, it does not mean that the resultant seedlings will be a combination of those six. Once a pistil has been pollinated it cannot be pollinated by subsequent pollen, and it seems highly unlikely that *C. × eriostemon* played any part in the breeding of '*jackmanii*'. Many subsequent crosses between various viticellas and lanuginosa bear witness to this, as their remarkable similarity show.

The only American species to be incorporated in clematis hybridizing is the scarlet-flowered *C. texensis* (see page 133), which was introduced into Europe in 1868, with the consequent introduction of red and pink colouring into clematis. In 1890, Jackman of Woking succeeded in crossing this species with large-flowered hybrids, thus producing semi-herbaceous climbers with tulip-shaped flowers, two of which are still in existence and much sought after.

As the popularity of clematis waned at the beginning of this century, hybridizing ceased, an occasional large-flowered hybrid appearing from time to time from unknown amateur raisers. It was not until the 1950s that more controlled hybridizing was begun, when the English hybridist Walter Pennell of Lincoln introduced 26 large-flowered hybrids, all mid-season varieties. I released my first hybrid in 1969, and since then have raised 22 clematis varieties at my nursery. The object has been to introduce more variety into the smaller flowered kinds and strength of growth into the larger flowers, a feature that is sometimes missing from some of the more recent introductions.

With the general growth in interest in gardening since the 1950s, particularly with the unavoidable trend to the smaller gardens, has come renewed appreciation of clematis and their use, especially in providing the third dimension, height. About a dozen standard varieties of clematis are generally available to gardeners, and these are almost invariably large-flowered hybrids with, probably, a montana or two and, possibly *C. tangutica*. An unfortunate aspect of this recent resurgence of popularity is that many garden centres and nurseries are responding to the demand with more enthusiasm than knowledge, and in many varieties are wrongly labelled. It is my hope that the following pages will provide more information for prospective purchasers.

CHOOSING A CLEMATIS

The general concept of clematis is that of climbing plants covering house walls and fences, arbours and pergolas, the latter perhaps associated more with large country gardens. The climbing habit certainly predominates in clematis, including all large-flowered hybrids and the great majority of species. They do so by twisting their petioles or leaf stalks around any suitable support. Other species, although non-clinging in habit, fully justify the tying-in that is required if they are grown against vertical structures, although they are also very effective if allowed to scramble through shrubs or trees, or, conversely, left to trail down banks.

However, another, smaller group consists of the less-well known herbaceous species, which is, perhaps, the most varied section in appearance and size, ranging as it does from statuesque, space-filling border plants to species with tiny flowers that invite close inspection.

Many first-time clematis buyers find it almost obligatory to ask for the universally known × *jackmanii* or 'Nelly Moser', often – and no disrespect is intended to these worthy varieties – because they are the only familiar names in an otherwise unknown territory. To see the full choice of large-flowered hybrids at a nursery, in flower at their peak time, is an eye-opener for many gardeners hitherto unaware of their existence and can, consequently, cause great deliberation, not to mention argument. Dismiss the idea that the colours range from blue-mauves to purples; there is a wide choice, from white, through pinks to various shades of red, quite apart from those with striped or shaded markings. Flower size can vary from the show-stoppingly large to the exquisitely tiny, which nevertheless display themselves in myriad forms to great effect. Amateur clematis gardeners divide roughly into three groups: devotees of the large-flowered hybrids only, those who have come to know and appreciate the species and accommodate both types, and finally those who have a natural affinity with the species to the exclusion of all others.

Space is the first factor to consider when you are choosing a clematis, and a greater awareness of how clematis can be used will increase considerably the space thought to be available. Even if space is thought to permit only two plants – for example, on the front wall of a terraced cottage – four can, in fact, be accommodated because two can be grown together. A judicious choice should take account of different heights of growth and flowering periods if two large-flowered hybrids are wanted for contrast, or staggered flowering times and pruning considerations if a large-flowered hybrid and a species are combined.

It seems so often to be the gardeners with restricted space who are the keenest and most imaginative, employing all possible means to grow these useful plants. They will have large containers displaying those varieties that are of more compact habit and eminently suitable for this purpose and give them that extra care that is required for all container-grown plants. There will be an archway, if not a pergola, for the charms, however momentary, of passing through a surround of flowers, and there will assuredly be herbaceous and semi-herbaceous types in every available spot. Where space is really at a premium, the predilection of the semi-herbaceous types for scrambling through a shrub is an extra advantage, making a double feature of a focal point in the garden. A montana may be draped on a wall or sufficiently sturdy fence; taken for granted for most of the year, it is a marvel in May. If there is room for just one tree, it can be adorned with a clematis; the viticella types are especially appropriate to small garden trees like rowans rather than the more rampant montanas, which can mantle large conifers.

Colour is always a personal choice, but suggestions are sometimes sought and even accepted. This is particularly true with the white-flowered types, whose showiness in the garden is sometimes doubted – quite without justification, for they are unsurpassed against the dark green of a conifer or holly, be they from the fine range of hybrids, whether dark-eyed or fair of face throughout, or one of the species clematis, whose flowers are tiny but borne in utter profusion.

Pale pink and silvery-lavender blooms can gleam most attractively if placed away from the sunniest parts of the garden; they are particularly suitable for a shadier wall or the darker green background of a shrubbery. These pastel colours in the species occur predominately in early-flowering ones, which are not subjected to strong sunshine. The brighter pinks and barred varieties of various colour combinations can usually state their case wherever they are placed, but for them in particular it is helpful to see a specimen before purchase rather than relying on a description in a catalogue.

Red clematis can be the hardest to place for best effect. Perversely sitting up and begging when in bloom, they are really best sited against light-coloured background walls; in the light, open position of a pergola or against a variegated, otherwise compatible shrub, the bright red colour can, surprisingly, be the least showy. There are a few light red blooms to which none of the foregoing applies – they mean to be seen.

If blue is accepted as being restful in terms of interior decoration, the same can be said in the context of clematis. There are numerous handsome and reliable varieties among the hybrids, nearly all distinguished by the sturdy male names common to many of the blue-flowered clematis. They vary from light blue to rich dark blue, but whatever the shade, blue is the most amenable colour for combining with other clematis or other climbers, except for the deepest colour in the clematis spectrum, purple. One could argue in half a dozen cases whether dark blue or purple is the appropriate description, but in either colour category there are instances that, having flowers of neither commanding size nor relieved by a light eye, do benefit most decidedly from the brighter contrast of another climber.

Flower size can be an important consideration in choice, although it is generally given the least attention. The term 'large-flowered hybrid' covers small, medium and large, the circumferences ranging from 4in (10cm) to 10in (25cm). The species, although on a smaller scale to start with, can nevertheless vary from $\frac{1}{2}$in (12mm) to 3in (8cm), their diverse shapes and flowering habits giving additional points to consider. Some of the large beauties among the hybrids show off even when contained in pots at a nursery; the smaller flowered species, on the other hand, appear less impressive unless they have been seen growing as specimen plants. A good catalogue, however, and a degree of imagination are rewarded within a year, when the profusion of small flowers show that they can hold their own in sheer dramatic effect.

There are other points to consider when choosing clematis. The majority of the species, and all the large-flowered hybrids, are deciduous, but a few species are evergreen and a delight, as any green covering in winter has to be. To have flowers as early as January, as can be the case with C. cirrhosa, is a luxury for any gardener. The facility for growing the evergreen types, apart from the most tender of them, is not always a straight north-versus-south decision, as the shelter afforded is the principal factor. As a group, they are as varied in flower and foliage as their deciduous counterparts.

Scent is an important consideration for many gardeners. Unfortunately, scent is not applicable to most clematis and consequently creates a great demand for those that do boast it. It will be no surprise that the scents are as diverse as all else to do with this genus and range from the hawthorn-scented C. × aromatica to the chocolate fragrance of C. montana 'Wilsonii'.

Texture of the flowers may not come immediately to mind, but familiarity with them makes one more aware of the difference. Given two flowers of not dissimilar colouring, it is surprising how a satiny sheen on one can make it more endearing; however, the rougher diamond may be a superbly reliable grower or able to resist wind-bruising to a greater extent.

Many gardeners start their collection of clematis after seeing a neighbour's spectacular specimen. They are fascinating plants on which many people (thankfully) become 'hooked' and about which they seek to extend their knowledge. These pages are intended to enable them to do just that.

CULTIVATION

There are the lucky few gardeners who need do no more than scoop out a trowel-sized hole just large enough to accommodate a clematis and, without more ado, have it grow like a weed and flower profusely. However, the great majority tend to garden on what can at best be termed uncongenial soil, and, even if you do have good garden soil, it is still worth that initial effort to try to bring the balance of success on to your side.

Before going into details of ground preparation, here are a few tips to consider when purchasing a new clematis. The first point is that it should be pot-grown. Occasionally clearance sales of bare-root plants are advertised. They are, at best, a risk, for clematis, particularly some of the species, resent root disturbance, and any reputable nursery or garden centre will offer them only in containers. If you personally choose your clematis, as opposed to buying by mail order, look for a bushy plant as far as possible, although some varieties by nature throw out only a single stem, a knowledge which can be gained only by experience. Go for plants with dark green foliage, not the sickly yellow, foot-high, drawn specimens sometimes offered. The roots should be coming out of the bottom of the pot, but the plant should not have been in the pot for so long that the surface is covered in moss. Purchases by mail order are virtually out of your hands, but advertisements offering strong three- to four-year-old plants really mean that the clematis have been in their pots for too long and are far from being a bargain. Again, plants offered as grown in 5–6in (12–15cm) pots give no indication of the size or quality of the plants; a well-grown clematis, of the correct size and age for planting, should have achieved all that is needed in an extra deep, 4–4½in (10–11cm) container. It is a good idea to ask friends or, even a complete stranger in possession of a good show of clematis where they were obtained. The proud owners will be only too pleased to tell you, and personal recommendation is, after all, a good nurseryman's trademark.

Autumn and spring are the best times for planting, although, as container-grown plants, they can be planted at any time throughout the summer as long as they receive frequent watering during any dry spells. Plants bought by mail order will undoubtedly be despatched in autumn as clematis, which start into growth early, will be too delicate by the spring to send through the post without damage.

It is a counsel of perfection in any literature on climbing plants to dig out a hole 18in square by 18in deep (46 × 46cm). That means 2 or 3 hundred-weights (approximately 100–150kg) of soil to be moved, and I doubt that anyone buying 10 clematis is going to take the trouble to move over a ton of their garden around. It is much more important to remember that you are making a home for a plant that should outlive its planter; quite a lot of clematis over 80 years old still give marvellous displays every year. Therefore, unless your soil is exceptionally good, remove as much as you can comfortably manage, about a cubic foot (0.03m³) if possible, and mix it with a generous amount of peat and a small amount of grit or sharp sand. Ideally, place a 2in (15cm) layer of well-rotted manure or garden compost in the bottom of the hole, put 2in (5cm) of the removed soil on top and dust with a good handful of bonemeal. Replace more soil until it reaches a level that will leave the top of the pot 2–3in (5–7.5cm) below ground level. This can be checked by standing the plant, still in its pot, in the hole; deep planting ensures that in the event of wilt or physical damage occurring, buds from below ground will shoot again.

If the plant feels dry before planting, place the pot in a bucket with enough water to come two-thirds of the way up the pot and leave for one hour. If it is in a plastic-bag type of container, lay the plant on its side on the ground and slit the bag down the side and along the bottom with a sharp knife, so that the plant can be taken out in one piece. On no account try to knock a plant out of a polythene bag container; it is virtually impossible. Plants grown in rigid types of pot can, in theory, be tapped sharply in the upside-down position, when they should leave the pots. Not an easy procedure though, when the plant comes complete with a 3ft (90cm) cane, and it usually results in three separate entities of a cane still tied to the plant, one heap of compost and one pot. It is much easier to lay the plant on its side and to push it out with a piece of cane or stick through the drainage holes in the bottom of the pot. If it does not come away easily, cut with scissors or knife down opposite sides of the pot; do not ruin a plant costing pounds for the sake of a pot that costs only a few pence.

Place the plant in the centre of the hole or, if it is to grow against a wall, set it against the front edge of the hole, which will bring it about 12in (30cm) away from the wall. Never put a plant close up to a house wall as the soil immediately there is dust-dry. A large-flowered hybrid will undoubtedly have its long whitish, bootlace-like roots wound round the bottom of the pot; carefully untangle some of these without disturbing the soil ball and spread them over the bottom of the hole. Species clematis and the small-flowered hybrids with fibrous root-systems are very susceptible to root damage and should not be disturbed in any way. Replace the rest of the soil, mix in a handful of compound fertilizer, such as John Innes base, or blood, fish and bone and firm round the plant. Water in well and, while the ground is still moist, top with a 2–3in (5–7.5cm) deep mulch of well-rotted manure, compost or peat.

Clematis like a rich, cool and moist root run, but will not tolerate one winter with their feet standing in water. On heavy, sticky clay that is otherwise sufficiently drained for the hole not to retain water, replace the removed soil with John Innes Potting Compost No. 3 and the plants should do fine. On the other hand, if the clay is of the type that makes a watertight sump, the clematis will rot away; in this situation consider whether it is worthwhile laying drains from each planting hole or whether it is better to forget about clematis altogether.

There are various ways of achieving the necessary cool root run. Where a paving slab has been removed in order to plant a clematis, no more needs to be done as this is the ideal situation, and the roots will soon find their way under the rest of the paving. In open borders and large beds, a thick mulch, paving slabs or large pebbles will help to keep the ground cool and moist. Another, and in many ways an ideal, method is to plant a low-growing shrub to cast shade over the root area or to set small leafy plants around the base of the clematis. For clematis growing against walls I make use of helianthemums a good deal as they make large flat mats from a central rootstock. These mats can be lifted up in order to feed and mulch the clematis, which is not the case with pebbles and stones, and ground-cover plants make less comfortable bases for marauding slugs than slabs laid on the ground.

Clematis are not self-clinging, but hoist themselves aloft by wrapping their leaf stalks round any support of suitable diameter. Plants growing against a wall must be provided with a support system; against stone or brick walls it is hard to better galvanized wire, fastened with vine eyes 2–3in (5–7.5cm) from the wall and strung in 12in (20cm) squares. It is visually unobtrusive, and I have never had trouble with scorching from hot wires. Colour-washed walls present a different problem, but panels of cedar wood trellis can be screwed on to blocks so as to give clearance from the wall; they can be taken off and bent down to the ground, clematis and all, during decorating. Although you can use mid-season and early-flowering clematis in these circumstances, it is wiser to choose the later-flowering varieties as these can be virtually cut to the ground in spring making life and decorating a lot simpler.

Whatever kind of support is used, tie the stems in place at intervals, at the same time training them in the direction in which you wish them to grow.

'I'm afraid I have no room for any more clematis, I'm completely out of wall space,' is a comment I hear many times. This need not be true, for if gardeners stopped to consider how climbers hoist themselves to the light in their natural habitat, a whole new area of gardening would be opened to them. In the wild, most clematis scramble over scrub or small shrubs, and some of the stronger species climb into trees. Most of the trees and shrubs in our gardens can accommodate a clematis of some kind, preferably the species or their immediate hybrids. It is best to plant clematis on the north side of the host tree as this is the cooler and more moist position; it will make its own way to the south and sun to flower. The usual recommendation is to plant the clematis on the outer extremity of the host tree and lead it in to the outer branches on a long cane or rope. This method is visually unattractive and means you must forever watch out for a slender stem when working in the garden. The position is also where the feeding roots of the tree are located and the carefully prepared site for the clematis will be just an *hors d' oeuvre* for the tree. Although the soil is drier at the base of the trunk, there are no feeding roots here, and it is easier to take a cane straight up the trunk. The varieties most suitable for growing into shrubs and trees are mentioned in the individual descriptions, but generally only the montanas can hope to compete with a large tree. Anti-social trees like ash, sycamore, large cherries and willows are best left to themselves.

Once the clematis is planted and growing well, there is a tendency to forget about feeding and mulching until the plant starts to deteriorate, and the flowers get smaller and smaller. Clematis are gross feeders and, if they are to produce the thousands of flowers of which they are capable, it is only politic to give a little in return for the amount of beauty that they bestow year after year. Each February or March work into the soil round the base of each plant one good handful of blood, fish and bone or John Innes base fertilizer, and mulch with a 2in (5cm) layer of garden compost or peat. Around the beginning of June give another handful of dry fertilizer or apply a liquid feed every three weeks throughout the growing season.

Water well in dry spells during the first year after planting; thereafter the root system will have ventured to seek moisture further down.

Pruning

More questions are asked concerning the pruning of clematis than about any other aspect; many amateur gardeners apparently feel that unless they prune they are missing out on some mysterious rite. Faced with the difficulty that some types need pruning at different seasons of the year and some must be cut back or thinned, while others need scarcely any pruning at all, it is little wonder that refuge is sought by way of a general spring-time 'tidying-up', cutting back all growths that seem to be in the way, frequently without being at all sure that it is the right thing to do.

The problem is exacerbated by the practice of some gardening writers of copying what has been said before without taking the trouble to research if the information was applicable in the first place. Confusion arises because some publications still refer to the once-common practice, with no more validity then than now, of dividing large-flowered clematis into different categories, mainly for pruning purposes, according to the main, or probable, species that went into the plant's hybrid make-up. Thus, it is possible to find references to the lanuginosa, patens, florida, × *jackmanii* and viticella groups, and so on.

The simple truth is that if no pruning was carried out at all, the plants would still grow and flower profusely, though not necessarily where you would want them to. They would be either somewhere high out of sight or eventually end up as a huge tangled mass, blocking the path or doorway without any semblance of order. Sound and orderly pruning advice is help-ful, but if instructions are followed too slavishly, without the exercise of common sense and observation, and all plants are treated alike, some will succeed while others will fail. In order to get the best from any one clematis it is necessary to take into acount the particular variety and the way in which it grows. Some have stiff upright growth, others have slender spreading stems; some are vigorous, others weak growers. Initially, this sounds a little per-plexing, and has been made more so by the conflicting and complicated pruning methods that have been advocated. At the other extreme, catalogues giving as a pruning guide merely 'hard' or 'none' makes for an apparently easy life, but it is not that simple. For pruning purposes, clematis are usually divided into three categories, which are referred to in the descriptions that follow as Groups A, B and C.

Group A
All clematis in this category flower in spring, from April to May, from dor-mant flower buds in the leaf axils on shoots that were produced during the previous season. It follows that any growth that is removed between late autumn and early spring will result in the loss of that same amount of flower for that season. Representative of this group are the popular montanas and the macropetalas.

There are thousands of montanas that have never been approached by secateurs or knife and that, every spring, make the most incredible waterfalls of bloom. Where these grow into and over a large tree, and *C. montana* and *C. vitalba* are the only ones capable of doing this, there is nothing you can do about pruning. However, where these strong growers are planted to cover some eyesore, like an oil tank, or are outgrowing their allotted space, it soon becomes apparent that some form of pruning is needed if this exuberance is to be curbed. *C. montana* and its close relatives, and *C. armandii*, throw out pencil-thick trails many yards long. First-time pruners probably find it satisfying to hold great bunches of cable and cut them through. Not so with

C. macropetala and *C. alpina* varieties, whose thin, wiry growths are like balls of twine that a cat has been playing with and defy detection as to where the plants start and end.

All of these, even the evergreen *C. armandii* (which many writers say does not need to be pruned), can be cut back as hard as is wished and as soon as possible after flowering. This should be no later than the end of July, which will give time for new growth to be made and ripen so as not to miss the next season's flowering. I know of two instances where very large armandii were cut right down to ground level and within two years were back to roof level. However, I would try not to cut into really old trunk-like growth at the base; such plants are likely to take exception to this and depart for ever. Some of the more tender evergreens, like *C. cirrhosa, C. indivisa* and *C. afoliata*, may be cut back by frosts, and the removal of all dead growth about April is all the pruning they are likely to need. Other types that come into this category are marked with A in the individual descriptions.

Group B

This group is sometimes divided into two sub-sections, the first covering the large-flowered hybrids, which flower *en masse* in May and June. They are borne on short growths, with one or two pairs of leaves, terminating in a single flower, followed by a lighter crop of smaller flowers in September and October. These are exemplified by such varieties as 'Nelly Moser', 'Barbara Jackman' and 'H.F. Young'; all the double-flowered varieties also belong in this category.

The other sub-section is typified by varieties such as 'W.E. Gladstone', 'Belle Nantaise' and 'King Edward VIII'. They usually have fewer flowers than the former sub-section, but make up for this by their extreme size, measuring 9–10in (22.5–25cm) across; from June until autumn they produce their flowers at the end of long growths. Some of these are rather tall, straggly growers and are ideal for climbing among climbing roses and tall wall shrubs. As all the clematis in this group require the same pruning treatment, it does not matter if you do not know the name of a particular plant, which you may well have inherited with the property.

A long-neglected plant of this group can be brought back to new life by cutting away all the top growth until you can see some kind of recognizable outline; the stems can then be trained and tied in as for a young plant. In the first spring after planting, cut the stem right back to just above a pair of buds, about 12in (30cm) from ground level. The ensuing shoots that arise should then be taken horizontally to the left and right of the main stem; this method will produce far more shoots to train up the wall than the 'pinching out of the tips' method usually advised. Even after so many years the rapidity with which new shoots will grow away never fails to amaze me. If you do not separate and tie in the stems, they shoot skywards in one great rope and the whole exercise will have been a waste of time. From the second year onwards, cut out all dead wood and very spindly shoots during February and March. The rest of the stems should be cut back to the topmost pair of large, fat green buds, which may be anything from a few inches to 1–2ft (30–60cm) from the tips of last year's growth. Snip these shoots free from their support, spread them out and retie them so as to cover and flower over as large an area as possible.

Group C
This group contains those clematis that must be pruned more severely than any others but that are also the easiest to prune. All too often one sees *C. × jackmanii* or a similar variety swaying disconsolately in the breeze, its large tangled mass of hair held high in the air over 8–10ft (2.4–3m) of lanky brown body. Any clematis that carries all its blooms on the current season's growth and that normally has a flowering period between late June and October will fall into this category, examples being *C. × jackmanii*, *C. viticella*, *C. flammula* and *C. orientalis*. Most, although no hard and fast rules can be given, grow tall, making between 10 and 20ft (3–6m) of growth in a season. In the case of the viticella and jackmanii types, and some of the species, the flowers occur on the final few feet of growth. As the majority of these start new growth in the spring within a short distance of the previous year's growth, it is obvious that soon they will grow out of sight or into a tangled mass if nothing is done to curtail them.

With clematis grown on walls or pergolas, simply cut through the entire bundle of stems to one node above the previous year's growth, during February or March. Pull away all of last year's old flowered wood and do not worry about the big green, healthy-looking buds or shoots that you will have to cut away – they will soon be replaced. By the very nature of this type of pruning, the length of old, bare stem will gradually increase over the years; this cannot be avoided and offers the opportunity to plant another low grower to hide the bare legs.

A number of the clematis in this group are eminently suitable for growing through trees and shrubs; indeed, they look far better that way. Prune clematis growing among small shrubs as for wall-trained types; those growing 8ft (2.4m) and more upwards can be left as they are, provided that the hosts can support them, or they can be cut back to about head height from the ground.

There are a few clematis that for ease are slotted into this group but that, in practice, sit rather uncomfortably astride the B and C fence. In the individual descriptions they are indicated as 'B/C', and examples include 'Mrs Cholmondeley', 'Hagley Hybrid', 'Niobe' and, in fact, all the red large-flowered hybrids. If we treat them as Group C and cut them hard back, they will flower very well on their young growth in late summer and autumn. However, were they to be pruned less severely, as in Group B, they would start to flower in May with even larger flowers, and with the added virtue of flowering spasmodically right through until late summer. The disadvantage, not to say the dilemma, is that as they keep throwing out long shoots from near the ends of the previous year's growth, the flowers and the leaves grow further and further away, with the bottom few feet of naked vine following closely behind. The only satisfactory method of dealing with these is to cut them hard back one year and prune lightly the following year, or to treat each plant as two separate halves and cut each half hard back in alternate years.

PROPAGATION

It is immensely satisfying to be able to increase plants from existing stock, in order to augment or replace a favourite variety or to exchange with friends. The amateur gardener usually requires only a few more plants for either eventuality, and while there are various ways of increasing clematis, there is only one foolproof method – and the easiest at that: layering. Autumn is the best time as the ground is likely to stay moist for the next six months. Remove from its support a stem long enough to lie flat along the ground; avoid any of soft green growth and choose instead one of the shoots produced earlier in the year, or even one from the previous year's growth. The chosen stem can be pegged down directly into the open ground, but it is more convenient to layer it into a 6in (15cm) clay pot sunk into the ground and filled with a mixture of equal parts sand and peat.

Your stem selected, make a slanting cut, about 1½in (4cm) long, on the underside, just behind the chosen node. Press this into the prepared pot, holding it in place with a bent piece of wire. You can layer from just one node or, if the trail is long enough, from several nodes along the stem (serpentine layering), although I find that a better root system is established if just one plant is propagated from each trail. Keep the potting mixture moist at all times. The layer should have rooted in 12 months, when it can be severed from the mother plant. Tie the new plant to a cane before lifting it out of the ground and transfer it to its new position.

The majority of clematis can be increased in this way, but for those that do not lend themselves to layering, other vegetative propagation methods can be used.

Division
Any large, old plant can be divided or have pieces split off from the main rootstock, but it is mainly herbaceous kinds, such as *C. heracleifolia* and

Peg down the selected stem into a clay pot sunk into the ground

C. integrifolia, that can be treated in this manner. In early spring, before new growth commences, chop off pieces from the outer edges of the plant, complete with crown buds and roots, and plant them straight out in their permanent positions.

Grafting

When I first started to grow clematis, about 80 per cent of all young plants were produced by grafting and 20 per cent from cuttings. During the last 20 years there has been a gradual reversal, and few plants are now grafted. However, some clematis are virtually impossible to propagate from cuttings, and I still resort to grafting to produce these. It used to be thought that grafting produced weak plants prone to wilt and to throwing suckers from the rootstock below ground, but the grafting technique of clematis differs considerably from that used for other plants such as roses and fruit trees. Here the rootstock provides the permanent root system for the grafted scion or top growth; the clematis rootstock, which usually consists of a two-year-old seedling of *C. vitalba*, is used only as a nurse stock to start the scion off. Within a matter of months, this will have grown its own root system, and the original rootstock will die away, the end product being not in the least bit different from one grown from a cutting. Few amateurs are likely to attempt grafting, if only because of the lack of suitable rootstocks, but the method may prove of interest.

To graft clematis, bind the scion and rootstock together with raffia

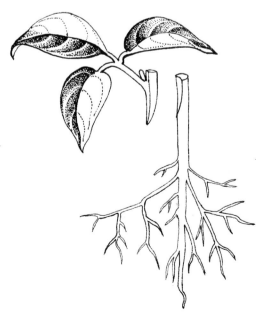 

Choose a seedling of *C. vitalba*, about $\frac{3}{16}$in (4–5mm) thick, cut across the top just below the cotyledons; using a sharp knife, cut a thin sliver, about 1in (2.5cm) long, from one side and cut an equivalent sliver from the chosen scion consisting of one leaf complete with dormant bud. Fit the two cut surfaces together, matching the cambium layers, and bind with raffia. Put the grafted plant in a small pot of moist potting compost, burying the union, and place it in a closed frame for four weeks, after which it can be gradually hardened off. The best time to do this is in the early spring. An expert will be successful with 100 per cent of the grafts.

Cuttings

Many, many clematis are now produced annually from cuttings, but you should not take this as an indication that they are easily propagated by this method. Although some clematis, the montana and orientalis groups, for example, are easily rooted from cuttings, the majority are by no means easy, some are difficult, and others are near impossible.

A clematis stem indicating divisions for cuttings

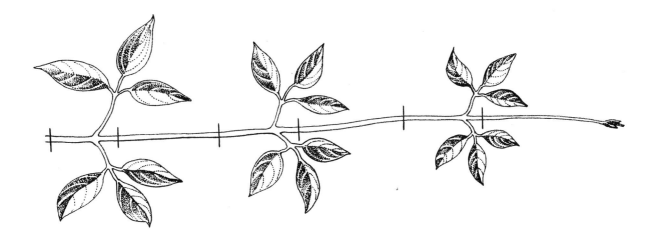

If you wish to attempt this method of propagation, use half-ripened shoots of the current year's growth. In late spring, cut through a selected shoot just below and also just above each node. Remove half the leaves and insert the cuttings in pure sand in the base of a cutting frame. Alternatively, the cuttings can be placed in a plant pot inserted in a clear polythene bag and kept in a warm, light place, but out of direct sunlight. Keep the cuttings moist, and, after four to six weeks, they will be ready to be potted separately into small pots.

DISEASES AND PESTS

Fortunately, clematis suffer far less from the many complaints that can beset other garden treasures. On the other hand, clematis wilt, the only major problem likely to be encountered, is a serious and frustrating complaint. This fungus disease has been the cause of much anguish and disappointment for clematis growers for well over 100 years, and, sad to say, we are not a great deal closer to solving the problem. As long ago as 1915, the New York Agricultural Experimental Station isolated the fungus *Ascochyta clematidina* as a cause of leaf-spotting and stem-rot. Growers in Britain had to wait until the 1960s for the Glasshouse Crops Research Institute at Littlehampton, Sussex, to verify the fungus, which had been found on wilted plants in this country. Recent research in Holland suggests another fungus, *Coniothyrium clematidis-rectae* as a possible cause of wilt. Christopher Lloyd, in his book *Clematis*, dismissed this on the basis that the fungus is not present in Britain, but it is fairly widespread, and whether this, or a combination of the two, is to blame we have yet to find out.

Another unexplained perplexity is why the disease is a major problem only on the large-flowered hybrids; it rarely affects the small-flowered hybrids, and I have never known any of the species troubled by it. However, *C. armandii* and related evergreens are sometimes attacked by *Ascochyta*, which causes leaf-spots and girdles of complete nodes, resulting in die-back above these points, but the disease is not severe enough to cause serious concern.

Clematis wilt can occur at any stage of growth, from a few feet onwards, and one or all of the stems may be affected. However, the most usual time of attack is when, after you have been daily watching the swelling flower buds with eager anticipation and expecting them to open the next day or at least the day after, suddenly there limply hangs the plant, leaves as well as flower buds; over the next few days stems, leaves and buds gradually change to dark brown.

If we knew the mode of attack by the fungi we would, at least, have a starting point for a cure for clematis wilt; as it is, we can only work within the confines of the scant knowledge available. In practical terms, this means treating the plants before attack occurs, as nothing can revive a plant once the symptoms have been noticed. Watering the base of the plant and the soil around the growing area with benomyl at $\frac{1}{4}$oz to 3 gallons (7gm to 14 litres), has given very reasonable results, and, although it cannot be guaranteed to banish wilt from the garden altogether, it will ensure that a major proportion of your clematis survive and prosper.

If a clematis does contract the disease, cut down and burn the offending eyesore. This harsh treatment will have very little effect on the eventual appearance of new shoots from below ground level – and reappear they will, for no matter how frustrating clematis wilt may be, it rarely proves fatal. New shoots from below ground may show within a matter of weeks, so that the only result may be a later show of flowers. On the other hand, your clematis may not show its head again for another year – I have even known plants come back to life after three years – so do not dig it out; clematis are notorious survivors.

The other major problem likely to affect your clematis is mildew. The trouble with mildew is that some years you may not see a sign of it in the garden; the following year, it can descend almost overnight, coating leaves and flower buds alike with a fine, milky veil. Just as some years may bring worse attacks than others, so areas and even individual gardens may be more prone to mildew than others. In addition, some varieties, × *jackmanii*, for instance, the late flowerers with viticella blood and the texensis hybrids, are more likely to be afflicted than other types. As the signs of mildew rarely appear before July or August, these late-flowering plants bear the brunt of the attack just when they are about to come to their peak.

If mildew were nothing more than an unsightly whitish wash, it might be classed as an 'acceptable' disease. Left unchecked, however, it can become terribly disfiguring, distorting leaves and flower buds so much that they fail to open – and those that do are grotesquely covered in a grey-white powder.

There is no excuse, however, for ever reaching the final stage described above. Mildew is easily controlled if you spray, as soon as the first signs are noticed, with a proprietary mildew fungicide. They are readily available, in wettable powder or liquid form; some of the powder-based fungicides leave a fine deposit on the foliage, so if you prefer a cleaner-looking plant, use triforine.

Two major pests, earwigs and slugs and snails, attack clematis, but slugs and snails are the most devastating if only for the reason that they are always with us. We are never going to eradicate them and the battle becomes a matter of control rather than elimination.

Apart from the obvious signs of slug damage where leaves are destroyed and young shoots are eaten into or, in a bad infestation, completely de-voured, leaving little round stumps, it is not often realized that slugs will take the bark from two and three-year-old stems. If you notice that more mature stems are taking on a smooth, silver-grey appearance, it is most certainly slugs, or snails, which are even more fond of debarking. Snails also tend to do more damage to open flowers, probably because they are hiding at that height and do not have far to travel; they are particularly troublesome where plants are trained on an old stone wall with plenty of daytime hiding places.

The proprietary products for controlling slugs and snails are so good that there is no excuse for bemoaning the fact that plants have been eaten away. Such pellets are of no use for old stone walls with lots of the mortar missing; the snails that sally forth on nightly forays from these cosy homes are not going to come down for the pellet type of bait. Instead, spray all over the wall with a proprietary liquid and you will be amazed by the number of dead snails, indicating how many a wall like that can harbour. It is of particular importance to keep a ring of slug pellets round herbaceous clematis, which have to fight the enemy afresh every spring.

Like slugs, earwigs are denizens of the night, usually unseen, only the remains of their nightly banquets greet us in the morning. Their leftovers seem to cause great argument among new gardeners as to what little beast has feasted. While earwigs do not kill a plant or even debilitate a strong grower, it is their liking for the one thing that we have waited all year to see, the flowers, that makes their attentions so devastating. So fond are earwigs of flowers that not only do they reduce fully open blooms to lacy tatters, but they will also bore neat round holes into the side of immature buds and gain entrance to eat out all the stamens from the inside. The leaves do not escape either, with only the tougher veins remaining.

Earwigs spend the earlier part of the year feeding on insects and turn to vegetable matter only in the latter half of the year. For this reason, early-flowering clematis are not troubled, and you will not see much damage before July. However, after a dry summer especially, they can be a menace. The most efficient method of treatment is a dusting of BHC powder, best applied when the foliage is damp with late evening condensation; one dusting is usually enough.

Occasionally, greenfly and blackfly infest the tips of growing shoots; they are readily destroyed with any proprietary aphid killer.

Mice may eat both flower buds and swelling growth buds; they are fairly easy to control with traps or poison bait. Bank voles, which have been known to chew the bark from quite large stems at ground level, are not so easy to control. They will not touch the usual poisonous cereal-based baits, and the only method I have had any success with has been a mouse trap baited with a green pea.

In built-up areas house sparrows peck out flower buds from clematis as they do from other plants. If damage is severe or persistent, spray with a bird repellent.

Late spring frosts can kill the tiny swelling flower buds on montanas. There is no defence against such acts of nature; it is merely an explanation of why some montanas fail to flower.

The following descriptions are divided into two major sections: large-flowered hybrids, and species and small-flowered hybrids. Each entry lists the accepted name, the hybridizer or country of origin where known, and the year in which the clematis was introduced. The letters A, B or C refer to the appropriate pruning category (see pages 18–22).

LARGE-FLOWERED HYBRIDS

Ascotiensis

Hybridizer unknown, 1871

The predominant colour among the mid-season hybrids is blue or a bluish shade. Not so with the late-flowering varieties, and we have had to make the most of the only two that have been available.

This is large for a late flower, 5–6in (12.5–15cm), and looks you in the eye rather than being of a nodding habit as a true jackmanii type. Starting with a fair amount of warm mauve in the blue, it soon changes to a good, clear mid-blue. The four, five or six sepals taper to points and are slightly wavy. The filaments are white, and the beige anthers, which look quite golden when caught in the sunlight, are large for a late variety; it is normally the earlier flowering hybrids which are associated with spectacular stamens. The leaves are heart-shaped, ternate and solitary. 'Ascotiensis' may start flowering as early as June and will continue into September.

Flowers: July–September
Height: to 12ft (3.6m)
Pruning category: C

Pages 30–1: 'John Huxtable'; below: 'Ascotiensis'

Opposite: 'Barbara Dibley'

Barbara Dibley

Hybridizer: Jackman

An elegantly shaped flower of a colouring that is most difficult to describe; the newly opened blooms are a gorgeous deep purple-red, with deeper coloured mid-ribs, which become more noticeable after a couple of days, almost putting it into the striped category. The colour can fade quite quickly to a rather tired blue-magenta; for this reason, 'Barbara Dibley' is best grown in partial shade. Until recently it was the sole representative in this colour range and it is still the best.

It is a moderate grower, not inclined to bush out to the side but of slender habit. The ternate leaves are rather large. The flowers, 8–9in (20–22.5cm) across, tend to look smaller as the eight long and tapering sepals recurve slightly at the tips with a gap between each. The anthers are dark red; the filaments are red shading to white at the base.

Flowers: May–June
Height: 6–7ft (1.8–2.1m)
Pruning category: B

Barbara Jackman

Hybridizer: Jackman

A love of mine for more than 20 years and a plant that I unhesitatingly recommend time after time, 'Barbara Jackman' is one of those that achieves that seldom-found combination of shape, colour, growth and freedom of flowering.

Vigorous and bushy with ternate leaves, it bears aesthetically pleasing flowers, each with eight broadly overlapping sepals that taper sharply to the tips. The 4in (10cm) wide flowers start as a lively, deepish purple-blue with a bright magenta bar that merges softly into the surrounding colour, making for fine contrast with the large creamy-yellow stamens. It fades gracefully to light mauve-blue with narrowed crimson midribs, and often gives a second, scattered display in the autumn.

Flowers: May–June
Height: 8ft (2.4m)
Pruning category: B

Beauty of Worcester

Hybridizer: Smith, c.1900

A wonderful, intense deep blue, admittedly with some purple in the colour, but even after 90 years, few hybrids can compare with this depth of colour.

The outer guard sepals, usually six in number, are surmounted by layers of smaller sepals, giving a large, flattish, slightly domed double flower 5–6in (12.5–15cm) across. These arise from short side-shoots from the previous year's growth. Flat, six-sepalled flowers are produced intermittently later and throughout the remainder of the season until stopped by autumn frosts. The creamy-white stamens create an unmistakable contrast. The leaves are heart-shaped, single and ternate. Unfortunately, the freedom of flowering associated with this clematis is not repeated in its growth habit, most new shoots running to flower after only two or three nodes. These compact growers are, however, ideal for covering the unsightly legs of, for example, climbing roses.

Flowers: May–June, and September
Height: 5–6ft (1.5–1.8m)
Pruning category: B

Bees Jubilee

Hybridizer: Bees, 1950s

Some plants have that extra 'something' that appeals or attracts. This is such a one. Quite a few striped and barred varieties are available, some much more recent than this, but I keep my allegiance.

The flat, rounded flower is 7in (18cm) across, with eight overlapping round-ended sepals; the base colour of mauve-pink with a delicate silvery feathering towards each outer edge is overlaid with central carmine bars. The filaments are white, and the anthers reddish-beige. The leaves are solitary, ternate and heart-shaped, tapering to points.

While it is slow to get started, it is not a weakling as is sometimes stated. It needs a good site and plenty of feeding. Some clematis will give a reasonable account of themselves on half measures; this is not one of those.

Flowers: May–June, and August
Height: 6ft (1.8m)
Pruning category: B

Belle Nantaise

Hybridizer: Boisselot, 1887

A flower, at a size of 7–8in (18–20cm) across, that can only be described as elegant as anyone who were to see the true 'Belle' would agree. Unfortunately there are other pretenders to the crown, several other clematis being offered under this attractive name.

Although the individual sepals are wide, tapering towards the tips, the fact that there are usually only six, and these slightly concave with wavy edges, makes for a rather gappy flower. However, this rather accentuates the way that each sepal falls gracefully downwards. The colouring is a good, clear pale lavender-blue set off by a very large boss of pale cream stamens. The leaves are simple and ternate. A good, moderately strong grower, it will not overwhelm with flowers in one major display but produces over a long period.

Flowers: June –August
Height: 10ft (3m)
Pruning category: B

Belle of Woking

Hybridizer: Jackman, 1875

This is a complete contrast to the large, single-flowered hybrids. The colour is a very soft silvery-mauve changing to silver-grey. There are no guard sepals, and the fully double, pompon-shaped flowers are only about 4in (10cm) across. The flowers tend to come in one early display but, as is usual with double flowers bereft of guard sepals, any later blooms will also be double. The

Opposite above: 'Barbara Jackman'; opposite below: 'Beauty of Worcester'

'Bees Jubilee'

stamens, which are not very conspicuous, are cream-coloured; the leaves are simple and rounded.

Although a moderately good grower once established, 'Belle of Woking' tends to be slow to get going. I also find that the neck of the stem is not really strong enough to carry the flower head as well as it should.

Flowers: June–July
Height: 6ft (1.8m)
Pruning category: B

Blue Diamond
Hybridizer: unknown

The unusual shape of the flowers always gives the impression of large, light blue butterflies clinging to the wall, from the distinctive manner in which each of the six wide sepals are convex along their length and then turn upwards to the tip. As the sepals are also slightly wavy along the margins, this creates a very pretty effect. The stamens are large and cream-coloured; the foliage mostly solitary. This variety appears to have disappeared from cultivation; even Fisk, which introduced it, no longer lists it. 'Blue Diamond' is a moderately good grower, which produces its flowers in two good displays.

Flowers: May–June, and September
Height: 6ft (1.8m)
Pruning category: B

Capitaine Thuilleaux
Hybridizer: unknown

Another striped variety, 'Capitaine Thuilleaux' was introduced from France by Fisk in 1969. The central bar of deep carmine-pink covers 50–70 per cent of the entire sepal, with just the outer edge being a silver-grey. There may be six or seven, but more usually eight, sepals, making a striking flower 7–8in (18–20cm) across. The filaments are white, and the anthers dark red; the leaves are ternate. This striking-looking flower tends to be only a moderate grower.

Flowers: May–June, and August
Height: 5–6ft (1.5–1.8m)
Pruning category: B

Opposite: 'Belle Nantaise'

'Chalcedony'

Chalcedony

Hybridizer: Strachan, 1984

The result of a cross between 'Vyvyan Pennell' and 'Marie Boisselot', the main characteristic of 'Chalcedony' is one of strength in the flowers, stems and foliage. There are no guard sepals, the 50–60 sepals being packed into a 5in (12cm) ball-shaped mass. They are strong and crisp to the touch, unlike those of 'Belle of Woking' (see page 34), which are soft and bruise easily.

This clematis is named after the semi-precious stone which, in its finer form, is of a translucent ice-blue, so similar in hue to the flower in question. The creamy stamens are not particularly conspicuous. The foliage is solitary and ternate, with large and leathery leaflets. Apart from being a good, strong grower, it is distinguished with a second autumn crop of flowers, which are also double although with fewer sepals.

Flowers: May–June, and September
Height: 8ft (2.4m)
Pruning category: B

Opposite: 'Belle of Woking'

Charissima

Hybridizer: Pennell, 1974

One of Walter Pennell's fine hybrids, a cross between 'Nelly Moser' and 'Kathleen Wheeler', 'Charissima' was given an attractive name, a fate that sadly did not befall the majority of Pennell's hybrids. The first impression is of a darker pink 'Nelly Moser', but there is more to this clematis than that.

Each flower, up to 7in (18 cm) across, has eight round-ended sepals, broad and overlapping and slightly wavy along the edges. The colouring is light cerise-pink, with a central bar of cerise-maroon, but the distinctive feature is that the veins over each sepal are in a darker shade, creating a beautiful netted effect, which becomes more pronounced as the flower fades. I prefer this softer, ageing bloom to the harder pink of the newly opened flower. The filaments are white to pink, the anthers dark maroon. The foliage is ternate, slender and tapering to sharp points. Altogether 'Charissima' is a fine plant, which grows well and is extremely free-flowering.

Flowers: May–June, and August
Height: 6–8ft (1.8–2.4m)
Pruning category: B

Opposite: 'Charissima'

Comtesse de Bouchaud
Hybridizer: Morel, *c*.1903

Justifiably one of the most popular clematis ever raised and, after 80 years, still the only self-pink that we have. Of a true jackmanii type, its 4–6in (10–15cm) wide flowers come in one great mass from the current year's growth. The six sepals are wide and very rounded on the ends, deeply grooved down the midribs, and the veins are also indented, creating a rather distinctive texture. They are slightly reflexed round the edges, with small, cream-coloured stamens. The foliage is divided into three to five leaflets.

A distinctive clematis, unlikely to be confused with any other, 'Comtesse de Bouchaud' is an easy plant, growing and flowering with equal abandon. It is not, however, a tall grower, and is, consequently, ideal for any situation of limited height.

Flowers: July–August
Height: 6–8ft (1.8–2.4m)
Pruning category: C

'Comtesse de Bouchard'

Corona
Hybridizer: Lundell, 1972

This particular variety is unlikely to be listed for much longer as it resembles 'Keith Richardson', an infinitely superior plant (see page 55), so much so that at times I cannot tell one flower from the other.

Each 7in (18cm) flower is composed of eight sepals of a similar purple-red to 'Barbara Dibley', but without the same depth of colour (see page 32). The filaments are white, and the anthers are dark red. 'Corona' is rather a low-growing plant, although it flowers well enough.

Flowers: May–June, and August
Height: 4–6ft (1.2–1.8m)
Pruning category: B

Countess of Lovelace
Hybridizer: Jackman, 1876

Until recently 'Countess of Lovelace' was the only double clematis of this colour, a mid-lilac-blue. Each 6in (15cm) wide flower has eight finely pointed guard sepals standing well beyond the lightly deeper shaded inner rows of layered smaller sepals. In complete contrast, the later crop of single flowers very often have

only six narrow, finely tapered sepals, but even so these are attractive in their own right. The stamens are pale, cream and small, the leaves are ternate.

Sometimes described as tricky, this clematis has always done well for me, and other plants that I have seen have confirmed its good qualities.

Flowers: May and August
Height: 6ft (1.8m)
Pruning category: B

Daniel Deronda

Hybridizer: Noble

The large flowers, 7–8in (18–20cm) across, are flattish, although each of the eight sepals tends to droop along the edges before tapering to a fine point. If the deep purple-blue colouring covered the whole of the surface, I could sustain a little more enthusiasm for this variety. However, the central midrib is of a decidedly washed-out greyish shade often combined with a strange, brownish-maroon shading. The stamens are creamy, the leaves are simple and ternate.

It grows well enough and flowers over a long period, although sparsely and without making any real impact. Occasionally, semi-double flowers are produced, but they are the exception rather than the rule.

Flowers: June–August
Height: 10ft (3m)
Pruning category: B

Dawn

Hybridizer: Lundell, 1969

This is a very pale pink, shading to a slightly deeper hue round the edges. The eight overlapping, blunt-ended sepals make for an attractive shape, 6in (15cm) across; the large boss of reddish anthers create a good contrast. It seems to grow and flower well enough, but leaves little to follow the initial flowering. It is essential to grow this variety out of the sun or it will be devoid of colour altogether.

Flowers: May–June
Height: 6ft (1.8m)
Pruning category: B

Dr Ruppel

Hybridizer: Ruppel, 1975

Since 1975 when Jim Fisk first marketed this clematis, it has become one of the better known of the modern varieties.

The flowers are large, up to 8in (20cm), and very attractively formed. The eight sepals overlap at the base and taper to sharp points with pretty crenulations along their length. The bright, rose-madder sepals are overlaid with central bars of deep carmine, and in the earlier flowers the bars can reach almost across the entire sepal. The autumn flowers, however, look little brighter than 'Nelly Moser'. The stamens are large and outstanding; the filaments are white, the anthers reddish-beige. The foliage is solitary and ternate. A good strong grower and very free-flowering, this is for you if you like strong colours. Some, however, may find it rather harsh.

Flowers:May–June, and September
Height: 6–10ft (1.8–3m)
Pruning category: B

Duchess of Edinburgh

Hybridizer: Jackman, 1875

One could almost describe this as a white 'Belle of Woking', so alike is it in flower form (see page 34). It has always been a popular clematis, doubtless because it is the only fully double white clematis available.

The flowers are not large, 4in (10cm) across, but they have depth, with the sepals tiered in rows one above the other, the stamens finishing off the centre like a little cream eye. Just below the flower head, encircling the stem, is a row of small leaflets on long stalks; they are usually green but may be mottled with cream and white. Here, at the base of the flower, the sepals do not seem able to decide whether they are leaves or sepals, and the amount of white mixed with green, or vice versa, varies from flower to flower and from season to season. Many writers have been disparaging about the green in what should be a white flower, but, from long experience of public reaction, I know that this feature seems to be one of its attractions.

The foliage, too, is certainly not to be confused with any others. Ternate and solitary, some, but not all of the leaves are irregularly lobed or incised and with double or treble points to the tips. The colouring is a yellowish-green, with the darker green veins creating a mottled effect.

It can be a good grower but is often difficult to establish, and even when it obliges, it is not particularly long lived in comparison with other varieties.

Flowers: May–June
Height: 5–6ft (1.5–1.8m)
Pruning category: B

Opposite above: 'Countess of Lovelace'; opposite below: 'Dawn'

'Dr Ruppel'

Duchess of Sutherland

Hybridizer: unknown

If I had to choose but one red clematis from among the large-flowered hybrids it would surely be this variety. Although there are only six sepals and these tapering to sharp points, they are wide enough to create a full, rather flattish flower about 6in (15cm) across. The rosy carmine-pink colouring is unlike any of the other reds and even fades pleasantly. Given only a light pruning, it will produce attractive, rather flat double flowers from the previous year's growth; the display is short, however, as the main flowering comes from the current season's wood, some of the blooms showing an extra sepal or two. The stamens are outstanding, being bright cream and contrasting extremely well. The leaves are ternate.

Two different 'Duchesses' are on offer from different nurseries, the other one being darker red with a lighter, greyish area along the midribs. The stamens, however, are still cream.

Sometimes described as being tricky to grow, my experience has always been that the 'Duchess of Sutherland' is a trouble-free plant.

Flowers: June, and August–September
Height: 12ft (3.5m)
Pruning category: B/C

Elsa Späth

Hybridizer: unknown

This extremely free-flowering plant produces masses of 8in (20cm) wide flowers in mid-summer and goes on to provide a second respectable display later on. The sepals are very broad and overlap, tapering sharply only at the tips and sitting very flat. Not really a blue – there is lavender-purple in its make-up – 'Elsa Späth' is a good deep colour, just lightening slightly down the midribs. The filaments are white, the dark red anthers tend to remain in an upright tuft, not opening out until the flowers themselves have been open for some days. The foliage is heart-shaped, tapering to long points. An easy plant, which grows well and flowers profusely.

Flowers: June–July, and September
Height: 6–7ft (1.8–2.1m)
Pruning category: B

Opposite above: 'Duchess of Edinburgh'; opposite below: 'Duchess of Sutherland'

Ernest Markham

Hybridizer: Markham, 1938

Two of the strongest growers among the large-flowered hybrids are to be found in the red group. This is one of those, producing plenty of foliage. Unfortunately, it is not quite so free with its flowers: in a cold, sunless spot it will probably bear none at all, but in full sun, it can be reasonably prolific. The flowers are a good bright magenta and although the six sepals have fine points, the general impression is of a rounded outline. Indentations along the veins give a rather textured look. The stamens, which are small and rather inconspicuous, are a warm beige. The foliage is divided into three or five leaflets.

Pruned lightly, it will start flowering in late June with large flowers, up to 6in (15cm) across, although not very many. It is one of the better known clematis, being available in most garden centres. In the right position it is an easily grown and striking plant.

Flowers: July–October
Height: up to 15ft (4.5m)
Pruning category: B/C

Fair Rosamond

Hybridizer: Jackman, 1871

During the last quarter of the 19th century, George Jackman raised a number of varieties having, as he phrased it, 'a decided fragrance'. Not all of them were named nor released and, of those that were, this is the only one remaining. To use Jackman's description, 'the scent is intermediate between violets and primroses', but while the scent of these plants can be detected some distance away, you will need to come a lot closer to 'Fair Rosamond'. The usual description of blush-white with pale red bar can be applied, but more often than not there is no bar and the blooms open pale blush, quickly changing to pearly-white.

A very prettily shaped, 5–6in (12–15cm) flower, the eight overlapping sepals have very fine points. The large boss of stamens make a fine contrast, the filaments shading from white to deep pink; the anthers are dark purple-red. A moderate grower, which flowers well, it does not offer much to follow after the initial display. The foliage is ternate, and the leaflets are narrow.

Flowers:May–June, occasionally again in autumn
Height: 6–8ft (1.8–2.4m)
Pruning category: B

Gipsy Queen

Hybridizer: Cripps, 1871

Although it is often confused with C. × jackmanii

'Superba', the distinctive rounded outline of the flower, created by the six sepals, rounded at the ends and tapering sharply to the base, makes 'Gipsy Queen' unlike any other clematis. The sharp tapering creates attractive kaleidoscopic cut-outs between the bases of the sepals, which measure 5in (12cm) across.

The deep, rich plum-purple colouring, combined with extremely vigorous growth and a flowering season extending over a three-month period, has made this one of the most popular clematis, leaving nothing more to be asked of it. The filaments are greenish-white; the anthers are dark red, and, although not showy, they are certainly more so than those on C. × jackmanii. The leaves are ternate.

Flowers: July–September
Height: 10–12ft (3–3.6m)
Pruning category: C

Hagley Hybrid

Hybridizer: Picton, 1956

Another of those awkward clematis that cannot decide which category to fall into. With light pruning 'Hagley Hybrid' will start flowering in June, bearing handsome, saucer-shaped flowers up to 6in (15cm) across. The main crop of 4in (10cm) flowers will come on the young growth and carry on virtually non-stop until October. The six boat-shaped sepals first open a pleasant pale mauve-pink; however, this colour is not even, being concentrated along the midribs and veins and creating a rather indeterminate effect, becoming more so as the flower quickly fades to a rather washed-out pink.

The large stamens form a good contrast; the filaments are white, the anthers purple-red. The leaves are ternate and rather sparse compared with most late-flowering varieties. Not a tall grower, it is vigorous enough and rarely out of flower.

Flowers: June–September
Height: 8ft (2.4m)
Pruning category: B/C

Haku Ookan

Hybridizer: unknown

'Haku Ookan' is the best of some recent introductions from Japan, most of which hardly seem to justify the effort of importation as they differ but little from existing varieties. The eight long, tapered sepals appear to be narrow as they tend to incurve along their length, creating a starfish-shape flower, 7in (18cm) across. The

Opposite: 'Gipsy Queen'

'Hagley Hybrid'

colour, a deep violet-purple, is further enhanced by a large boss of white stamens. The ternate leaves are solitary and dark green. Growth is only moderate, but it does have a respectable second flowering.

Flowers: May–June, and September
Height: 6ft (1.8m)
Pruning category: B

Henryi
Hybridizer: Anderson-Henry, 1858

This, and its sibling 'Lawsoniana', are probably the oldest large-flowered hybrids still in cultivation. There is a touch of cream in its white colour, but 'Henryi' has stood the test of time well considering that numerous white hybrids have disappeared from the scene. Its eight slightly overlapping, sharply pointed sepals sit very flat, forming a flower of classic outline 6–7in (15–18cm) in size. The boss of contrasting stamens is large and well-formed, the white filaments tipped with warm brown anthers. The foliage is ternate and solitary, quite large and leathery.

It has never caused me any problems, although it is known to be a prime wilter for some.

Flowers: June and September
Height: 6–10ft (1.8–3m)
Pruning category: B

Herbert Johnson
Hybridizer: Pennell, 1973

An extremely large-flowered hybrid, each bloom easily reaching 10in (25cm) across. The eight sepals are wide and overlapping, but are inclined to be floppy and rather heavy. The colour, a warm rosy-mauve, is pleasant enough, but somehow fails to come across. Even the stamens are hardly distinguishable as the dusty mauve anthers merge into the flower colour.

The foliage is large, solitary and ternate. Growth is moderate, but it flowers very well. A good if not inspiring clematis; I would have expected something better from the parentage of 'Vyvyan Pennell' and 'Percy Picton'.

Flowers: May–June, and August
Height: 6ft (1.8m)
Pruning category: B

Opposite above: 'Haku Ookan'; opposite below: 'Henryi'

H.F. Young
Hybridizer: Pennell, 1962

Without doubt 'H.F.Young' is one of Walter Pennell's finest introductions. There are no true blues in clematis, all having varying degrees of mauve mixed in with the blue, but here we have a flower as bright a mid-blue as is probably obtainable in a clematis. The flowers are large, up to 8in (20cm), and most attractively formed, the eight sepals wide and overlapping but not lying flat. The wavy edges impart a distinctly feminine look, if a flower can be said to have a masculine or feminine look, and I never look at this one with the name 'Horace' in mind.

The creamy-white stamens contrast rather well, and the mainly ternate leaves are neither too sparse nor too overpowering. Of moderate height, it bushes out well to the sides, never appearing leggy, and the flowers are evenly distributed from ground level. I have grown this variety since it was first introduced, and never was a plant more amenable.

Flowers: May–June, and September
Height: 8ft (2.4m)
Pruning category: B

'H.F. Young'

C. × jackmanii
Hybridizer: Jackman, 1863

Non-clematis lovers, non-gardeners even, can usually describe this plant so well known is it. This was the first flower to combine size with a deep purple colouring; actually bluish-purple with a slight reddish flush at the base. There are usually four sepals although there can be five or six, and they are slightly twisted and gappy; the 4–5in (10–12cm) flowers face outwards and downwards. The stamens are small, green and insignificant, and the leaves are simple and ternate, with five leaflets.

Still going strong and capable of putting on a good show; personally, I prefer C. × jackmanii 'Superba' (see below) which is the one most frequently offered by nurseries and garden centres.

Flowers: July–August
Height: 8–10ft (2.4–3m)
Pruning category: B

C. × jackmanii 'Alba'
Hybridizer: Noble, 1878

In the wake of the immense popularity of C. × jackmanii, it became good business sense to cash in on a well-known name. This variety was supposedly a hybrid

betwen *C.* 'Fortunei' and *C.* × *jackmanii*, but a plant less like *C.* × *jackmanii* would be hard to imagine.

A sparse crop of double flowers can be expected from the previous year's wood. They are about 5 in (12 cm) across, the outer sepals, which vary in length, creating a ragged effect. These are usually streaked with mauve and tipped with green, some to quite a large extent. The ground colour of very pale bluish-lilac is carried into the inner three or four layers, which also vary in length, the whole forming a rather untidy flower. The single, six-sepalled flowers, which come later, are far more attractive, the white colouring has a bluish wash and the veins a slightly deeper shade. The white filaments have light brown anthers. One of the strongest-growing hybrids, it has masses of large light green foliage. Without doubt the easiest of the large-flowered hybrids to grow, it is very good for a beginner.

Flowers: June–September
Height: 10–15ft (3–4.5m)
Pruning category: B/C

C. × *jackmanii* 'Rubra'
Hybridizer: Jackman

Yet another hybrid to take on the well-known name and, although it is nearer to its namesake than *C.* × *jackmanii* 'Alba', 'Rubra' still bears little resemblance to *C.* × *jackmanii*. Like 'Alba', 'Rubra', will produce double blooms from the old wood, given a light pruning. They can be large, up to 7in (18cm), if only a few are produced, with six tapered guard sepals surmounted by a rather unevenly layered inner dome of smaller, flattish sepals. These can be very striking, although if the early display is quite generous, the inner sepals, curled and wavy, are spread far more thinly and in a thoroughly disorganized way.

The main display of 5in (12cm) single flowers starts rather earlier than in some of this type, giving a long flowering season. On newly opened blooms, the crimson-lake colouring has a rich velvety texture; alas, this soon fades to a jaded bluey-beetroot shade, a colour I dislike, although many people favour off-beat shades. There are contrasting cream stamens, and the leaves are ternate.A good, strong free-flowering grower.

Flowers: June–September
Height: 12–15ft (3.6-4.5m)
Pruning category: B/C

C. × *jackmanii* 'Superba'
Hybridizer: Jackman, 1878

As free-flowering as the old *C.* × *jackmanii*, but the flowers are larger and the sepals broader, giving a much fuller-looking appearance. The colouring is similar, although the reddish flush extends more along the midribs, fading as the flowers age. Otherwise, growth and foliage are similar.

It has long been a vexation to me that the explanation of the origins of this variety have never accorded with my own observations of clematis behaviour. Said to have been produced as a sport from *C.* × *jackmanni* at the Woking nursery, it was only during my researches for this book that I may have inadvertently stumbled across the answer. The meaning of the term sport usually denotes the appearance of a stem or flower differing in some way from the original plant. If this is considered to be sufficiently different or superior, this portion is used for propagation, and so begins a new plant. Some plants seem only too willing to sport different coloured flowers – chrysanthemums and roses, for example – others virtually not at all. Clematis are in this latter category. Even if it did happen, by the time the flower was seen, the stem carrying this desired new flower would most certainly be too old and beyond propagation. However, a study of hybridizers' notes made around the turn of the century suggests that the term sport appears to have been used in a completely different context and was applied to seedlings from a variety that differed from the parent plant. This would explain how the term came to be used for *C.* × *jackmanii* 'Superba' when, in fact, it was produced as a seedling in the normal way.

Flowers: July–August
Height: 8–10ft (2.4–3m)
Pruning category: C

James Mason
Hybridizer: Fretwell, 1984

This cultivar is named after the late, renowned film actor who had such a passionate interest in gardening. A true Yorkshireman, he was extremely fond of white flowers.

Quite a few white-flowered varieties exist, but only one (and that not a true white) possesses dark stamens. This hybrid (from 'Marie Boisselot' × 'Lincoln Star') has large, 8in (20cm), flowers composed of eight wide sepals overlapping at the base and tapering to fine points.A good solid white, with three distinctive deep grooves along the midribs and attractive undulating edges, it is further enhanced by the very large boss of dark maroon anthers with white filaments. The foliage is solitary and ternate. It is a reasonably strong grower.

Flowers: May–June, and September
Height: 6–8ft (1.8–2.4m)
Pruning category: B

Opposite: *C.* × *jackmanii* 'Rubra'

John Huxtable

Hybridizer: Huxtable, 1967

Since the introduction of *C.* × *jackmanii* brought size to the autumn-flowering hybrids, it has been every clematis breeder's objective to produce a white variety with the same late-flowering characteristics, but always it seemed to elude them. In Britain, Smith's Nurseries of Worcester introduced 'Smith's Snow White Jackmanii' at the turn of the century, but this was yet another example of a rather vivid imagination being allowed too free a hand in the plant's naming.

Some time before I had overcome the problems of breeding a white clematis flowering entirely on the current season's growth, John Huxtable, who lived not far away from me in Devon, England, had raised a chance seedling from 'Comtesse de Bouchaud' (see page 41). Probably self-pollinated, as it so resembles its seed parent, 'John Huxtable' could be described as a pure white 'Comtesse'. The flower shape, size and foliage, habit of growth and time of flowering all follow closely in its dam's image.

As good a performer as 'Comtesse', it was always John Huxtable's regret that, for some perverse reason, this

'James Mason'

namesake of his would never grow in his own fine garden.

Flowers: July–August
Height: 6–8ft (1.8–2.4m)
Pruning category: C

Kathleen Wheeler

Hybridizer: Pennell, 1967

This is distinguished by large flowers, each 7in (18cm) wide, with eight sepals, wide and overlapping for half their length from the base and tapering to blunt tips. Very distinctive deep grooves run the length of the central rib, and this area is a deeper shade than the rest of the flower, which begins as plummy-mauve, gradually losing the rosiness but nonetheless, fading to a pleasant shade. The large stamens are outstanding, the lilac filaments shading to cream towards the creamy anthers. The leaves are solitary, ternate and lanciolate, with wavy edges.

A crisp-looking flower, which shows itself very well, its seed parent is given as 'Mrs Spencer Castle'. Although the pollen parent is unknown, it must have been vigorous as this is a good grower, bushing out well to the sides. You can expect a quite respectable second

flowering in the autumn; the flowers are smaller than those in the main display and usually have six or seven sepals.

Flowers: May–June, and August–September
Height: 8 ft (2.4 m)
Pruning category: B

Keith Richardson
Hybridizer: Pennell, 1975

In the description of 'Corona' (see page 41) I mentioned the close similarity to this variety: the same purple-red colouring, more blue round the edges being common to them both, and both without the depth of colour achieved by 'Barbara Dibley'. The eight sepals, wide and slightly waved, somehow give the impression that 'Keith Richardson' has a fuller flower than 'Corona'. On established plants, the flowers are larger, 8in (20cm) across, but they are not noticeably so on young specimens. The filaments are white, the anthers red, and the foliage is solitary and ternate. It is a stronger grower than 'Corona'.

Opposite above: 'John Huxtable'; opposite below: 'Kathleen Wheeler'

'Keith Richardson'

Flowers: May–June, and August
Height: 8ft (2.4m)
Pruning category: B

King Edward VII
Hybridizer: Jackman, c.1902

For many years, the clematis issued under this name has never matched the original description given by the raiser. During the summer of 1983 I was invited to visit the garden of a manor house in Devon, England, one-time home of a local family, the Grahams. One member of the family, at the turn of the century, had obviously been an avid gardener, and this once beautiful garden, now sadly overgrown, still contained some of the original clematis bought from Jackman in the early 1900s. The front of the house held the remains of some long-dead clematis plus one still-vigorous plant of 'The President'. However, the tall gable end was a sight to behold for here a plant of C. × jackmanii 'Rubra' had managed over the years to encircle an iron downpipe, some 15ft (4.5m) long. To the right of this was a clematis subsequently verified as 'King Edward VII', 15 ft (4.5 m) wide and around 25ft (7.5m) high, with flowers along the topmost growth and sheeted down to within 10ft (3m) of the ground. Jackman's original description of 'pucy-violet' with a reddish flush along the midribs fitted the bill admirably. I have never seen, and doubt that I ever will see, flowers larger than these. The largest measured 11in (27cm) and not one was less than 9in (23cm); even so they did not appear gross as the eight, sometimes six or seven, sepals taper to fine points and do not overlap. The filaments are greenish-white, with reddish-beige anthers. The large and leathery leaves are mostly ternate.

From the parentage given by Jackman – 'Fairy Queen' × *C. texensis* 'Sir Trevor Lawrence' – one would not have expected so large a flower, but that is the excitement of hybridizing. One wonders how such a strong grower, flowering over a long period from the tips of young growth, could ever fall from favour.

Flowers: June–August
Height: up to 25ft (7.5m)
Pruning category: B

Kiri Te Kanawa
Hybridizer: Fretwell, 1986

It is unfortunate that many of the older double clematis varieties, although beautiful, were rather weakly. It was with this in mind that I decided to try to produce varieties that had strength as well as desirability.

'Kiri Te Kanawa', which was raised from 'Chalcedony' × 'Beauty of Worcester', has both of these attributes in full measure; the crisp, stiff sepals are packed into round, solid dahlia-like flowers, each 5in (12cm) across. There are no guard sepals, which means that we have the chance to appreciate a second display of double flowers in the autumn. The colour is a good, deep blue, lacking the depth of colour of 'Beauty of Worcester' (see page 34) but without the purple in the colouring that pertains to that variety. The stamens are cream and below the flower is a circlet of rounded, mottled cream leaves, common to this kind of double flower. Moderately vigorous, it is very free-flowering.

Flowers: May–June, and September
Height: 6–8ft (1.8–2.4m)
Pruning category: B

Lady Betty Balfour
Hybridizer: Jackman, 1910

The parentage of this variety, 'Gipsy Queen' × 'Beauty of Worcester', gives some indication of the depth of colour to be expected. The newly opened flower is a deep, rich purple with a hint of red near the base, but this changes quite quickly to a deep rich blue. The six sepals are wide and overlapping, the entire flower being 5in (12cm) across. The cream-coloured stamens are large for a late-flowering variety and provide a fine contrast, while the ternate leaves are not overpowering as is sometimes the case with vigorous growers.

One of the most trouble-free clematis, annually throwing out masses of shoots, it is exceptionally free-flowering provided that it is sited in a sunny, warm spot, not because it is tender but because of the lateness of the flowers. This variety, which is so attractive in the right position, will, in a sunless one, hardly get into its stride before the autumn frosts, and moreover, if the flowers are too late they never achieve the same depth of colour.

Flowers: September–October
Height: 15ft (4.5m)
Pruning category: C

Lady Caroline Nevill
Hybridizer: Cripps, 1866

Although not to everyone's taste, I am fond of the clematis with pastel shades, and of this one in particular. The early flowers, which appear in May, are large, 7in (18cm), and semi-double, with one or two layers of smaller, flattish sepals surmounting the outer eight, wide and overlapping sepals, which taper to blunt points. The later flowers, from the current growth, are only marginally smaller but always single. The pale blue colour, with a hint of mauve, has a slightly deeper mauve-blue flush along the midrib, the whole surface having a smooth satin sheen. The filaments are white, and the anthers are rosy-beige. The simple leaves are ternate. An attractive, moderate grower, there is a good second flowering period.

Flowers: June and September
Height: 6–8ft (1.8–2.4m)
Pruning category: B

Lady Londesborough
Hybridizer: Noble, 1869

Another very pale variety, 'Lady Londesborough' is a pale pinkish-mauve, deeper around the edges and fading to an even paler silver-grey. The deep purple anthers form a fine contrast, the filaments being white.

The flowers are small for an early variety, no more than 5 or 6in (12–15cm). They have excellent form, each with eight wide sepals that are blunt-ended and

Opposite above: 'King Edward VII'; opposite below: 'Kiri Te Kanawa'

strongly overlapping. They tend to come in one massive display, covering the entire plant in early summer and leaving little to follow in the season. The ternate leaves are quite neat. A moderate grower.

Flowers: May–June
Height: 5–6ft (1.5–1.8m)
Pruning category: B

Lady Northcliffe
Hybridizer: Jackman, c.1906

'Lady Northcliffe' is one of the most popular clematis, chiefly noted for its excellence in hardly ever being out of flower between June and September, but even producing occasional blooms much later, until they too have to bow out to winter.

On the deeper side of mid-blue (admittedly with some lavender in the blue), the flowers, 6in (15cm) wide, have a distinctive outline, the normally six sepals being wide and overlapping, with large waves along the edges and not lying flat. The stamens are a duller cream colour than is usual. The foliage is ternate. As is usual with those varieties that expend most of their effort in flowering, the height tends to be limited, although growth is vigorous and healthy.

Flowers: June–September
Height: 4ft 6in–6ft (1.3–1.8m)
Pruning category: B

Lasurstern
Hybridizer: unknown

This popular variety bears extremely handsome flowers, the seven or eight sepals overlapping at the base, tapering to fine points and sitting flat with the edges themselves undulating. The flowers are large, 7in (19cm), and so numerous that they almost obliterate the foliage; they hold themselves well, neither hanging their heads nor looking to the stars. The deep blue colour does fade, especially along the central area, but always keeps a lively shade, the deep cream stamens providing excellent contrast. The ternate foliage is tapering and slightly wavy.

A strong grower, it is often described as having nothing to offer in the autumn. This has not been my experience and, if fed as it should be, a modest autumn display may be expected.

Flowers: May–June, and September
Height: 8ft (2.4m)
Pruning category: B

Opposite above: 'Lady Caroline Nevill'; opposite below: 'Lady Londesborough'

Lawsoniana
Hybridizer: Henry, 1855

As with 'W.E. Gladstone' (see page 84), the flowers appear towards the ends of long shoots, so it seems sensible to encourage horizontal growth rather than allow it to head skywards. The flowers are well formed even though they are 9in (23cm) across, with six to eight finely tapered sepals. Deep lavender in colour with quite an amount of pink on opening, it changes to pale lavender-blue. The filaments are white, and the anthers beige.

Flowers: June–September
Height: 10ft (3m)
Pruning category: B

Lincoln Star
Hybridizer: Pennell, 1954

There has always been a need for a pink clematis – a true pink, not bluish or mauve – and when this variety was introduced, the bright raspberry-pink colouring was unique among clematis. The early flowers can be up to 6in (15cm) across, although they appear to be much smaller as the eight sepals are narow, tapering to long points, leaving large gaps between each one.

It is in these early blooms that the bright pink is concentrated, covering most of the sepal except for a pale pink margin. The stamens are conspicuous, large and shapely, the white filaments tipped with maroon anthers. The later autumn flowers are, in contrast, considerably smaller and off-white in colour, with mottled, pale pink bars. The leaves are ternate, tapered and sparse. If only so much early promise came to fruition, but this is a weakly plant, not one to be planted in isolation but rather to hide the bare legs of some stronger relative.

Flowers: May–June, and August
Height: 4–5ft (1.2–1.5m)
Pruning category: B

Lord Nevill
Hybridizer: Cripps, 1878

The reason such an old variety remains popular is obvious when we realise that a flower of such an intense electric-blue has never been overshadowed after 100 years. The deep blue colour is even more concentrated along the veins, producing a pretty textured effect. The six, seven or eight sepals overlap at the base and taper to sharp points, the edges being attractively waved. Although the filaments are white, the anthers are deep

purple-red and provide no contrast; not that this matters, for it rather adds to the effect and we have plenty with cream stamens. Flowers are 6–7in (15–18cm) across; the foliage is ternate. A reasonably strong grower, there is a good second flowering in the autumn.

Flowers: June and September
Height: 8ft (2.4m)
Pruning category: B

Mme Baron Veillard
Hybridizer: Veillard, 1885

Along with 'Lady Betty Balfour' (see page 56) this shares the distinction of being one of the only two large-flowering hybrids that save their displays entirely for the autumn. The six sepals are very rounded at the ends and slightly reflexed; the bright rosy-lilac pink colouring is even throughout the flower, and the surface is strangely puckered, creating a textured effect. The stamens are small and pale greenish-cream. The leaves are ternate and rather too plentiful. The flowers, 4–5in (10–12cm) wide, are freely produced on very vigorous plants.

Flowers: September–October
Height: 15ft (4.5m)
Pruning category: C

Mme Edouard André
Hybridizer: Veillard, 1893

All the red clematis have a certain amount of blue in their make-up, and this variety starts with more than most. Although the wine-red colour fades, it does not change into that jaded, nondescript colour that detracts from others, such as C. × jackmanii 'Rubra'. The flowers, 5in (12cm) across, have a pretty saucer-shape, the six sepals tapering to fine points. They have a very matt finish, and while they are not at their most appealing on young pot-grown specimens, the variety should be judged in a garden context. The creamy stamens contrast well with the sepals. The leaves are ternate, adequate but not overpowering, and the same could be said for the growth habit.

Flowers: July–September
Height: 8ft (2.4m)
Pruning category: C

Opposite: 'Lady Northcliffe'

Mme Grange
Hybridizer: Grange, 1875

This is closely akin to C. × jackmanii, which is not surprising as they both have the same parentage. The differences become apparent on closer inspection. The newly opened flowers, 5 in (12 cm) across, are very distinctive, the six sepals rolling inwards along their length, revealing a woolly, greyish underside; eventually the sepals do flatten out. The deep purple is shot through with dark red, which is concentrated along the midribs. The reddish-beige anthers are hardly distinguishable. Leaflets appear in fives. A vigorous grower, it produces plenty of flowers.

Flowers: July–September
Height: 10ft (3m)
Pruning category: C

Marcel Moser
Hybridizer: Moser, 1896

This has the same mauve-pink ground colour, with carmine central bars, as the well-known 'Nelly Moser' (see page 70) and the stamens, too, are the same deep maroon. The shape, however, is totally different, the eight sepals being long, narrow and tapering to fine points, leaving gaps between the sepals. Arguably a nicer shape than 'Nelly Moser', the flowers of 'Marcel Moser' are marginally larger at 9in (23cm). The leaves are ternate, narrow and taper to long points.

'Marcel Moser' does not, however, have the same prodigious growth as 'Nelly Moser', and although it can eventually make a decent plant given plenty of feeding, I have always found it rather difficult and slow to get started; it has the same propensity to fade to nothing if grown in full sun.

Flowers: May–June, and September
Height: 6–8ft (1.8–2.4m)
Pruning category: B

Marie Boisselot (syn. Mme le Coultre)
Hybridizer: Boisselot, c.1900

I have always had a great affection for white-flowered plants, and for sheer impact the white-flowering clematis are hard to beat. Apart from C. montana, this hybrid must be the most commonly grown white, so much so that the average gardener could be forgiven for believing that it is the only one. Although numerous white clematis have been around for a longer period, and quite a few introduced since, none have managed to attain quite the dense whiteness of this one, even though the newly opening flowers have a lilac-pink flush.

Seed

Most of the more commonly grown species will set seed, which will germinate quite readily, although it will not, of course, reproduce the parent plant exactly. A few of the resulting plants may be an improvement, but most will be much poorer, as may be seen from the many poor forms of macropetala and alpina now offered for sale. If you have a good form, the best method is to reproduce by vegetative propagation. The species least likely to vary greatly from the parent is *C. tangutica*, and, if the seeds are sown in early spring, the plants can even be of flowering size by the autumn.

None of the hybrids (and this includes named varieties of the species) will produce seedlings that in any way resemble their parents. Unless you are embarking on a breeding programme with definite goals in mind, and are prepared to grow on to flowering size and then discard 99.9 per cent of the plants, it is better to forget the idea.

The flowers are large, reaching 8in (20cm); the eight sepals are very wide, overlapping so much that they reach the centre of the adjacent one, and create a rounded, inverted saucer-shape flower. The stamens are small and of little importance as their creamy-white colour is hardly noticeable. The leaves, quite large and rather too plentiful, are solitary and ternate, wide and heart-shaped. A good, strong-growing plant, and although it may not be covered with a profusion of flowers, there are enough of them. The plant may, if desired, be pruned hard in spring to produce a good single display of flowers in autumn; but I find those huge early show-stoppers one of the main attractions. If there is a fault here, it is that the flowers are held on a horizontal plane; ideally the plant should be sited in a position that ensures that it is not too much above eye level.

Plants identical to this may appear under the name of 'Mme le Coultre'; they are not a different variety, but are imported from Holland where 'Marie Boisselot' is better known as 'Mme le Coultre'.

Flowers: June–September
Height: 8–12ft (2.4–3.6m)
Pruning category: B

Opposite above: 'Lord Nevill'; opposite below: 'Mme Baron Veillard'

'Mme Edouard André'

Maureen
Hybridizer: unknown

Although this variety has been around since the 1950s, no one seems to have laid claim to its introduction. This is strange because it is one of the best of the post-war clematis and should be seen much more often. Each flower, about 6in (15cm) across, consists of only six sepals, but these are so wide as to completely overlap, not lying flat as the edges undulate slightly. The rich violet-purple ground colour is suffused with red, especially along the midribs, the whole flower having a gorgeous velvety texture with contrasting creamy stamens. The foliage is ternate and rather sparse.

Although the main flowering is on the current season's growth, and this can be maintained by hard pruning, it is not a very tall grower and with a light pruning only, it will start flowering in June and go on virtually non-stop.

Flowers: June–September
Height: 6ft (1.8m)
Pruning category: B/C

Miriam Markham
Hybridizer: Markham, 1939

Contrary to popular belief, Ernest Markham, who was William Robinson's gardener at Gravetye Manor, raised hardly any of his own varieties. This, however, was one of his and named after his wife a short time after his death. It is a personal favourite, certainly in my top 10, not for its vigour, which is only moderate, nor for its mass of flowers, for these are not numerous, although strategically placed. This is just as well for each bloom is so exquisite and would be spoiled by mass competition. The outer guard sepals, of a soft lilac shade and tapering to fine points, number eight, although often there are two equal-size layers of them. In four or five loose layers surmounting the guard sepals are shorter, quite wide sepals in a pleasant rosy-lilac, shaded in so subtle a way that it needs to be seen to be appreciated, and blessed with a silky texture. The filaments are pale green with rosy-beige anthers. The large leaves are ternate with some leaflets occasionally lobed.

The largest flowers will come in May from the previous year's wood and terminal flowers are produced progressively from the current growth. As I write this in early December it is still flowering, admittedly with a certain amount of green in the colouring.

'Marie Boisselot'

Opposite above: 'Maureen'; opposite below: 'Miriam Markham'

Flowers: May–October
Height: 6ft (1.8m)
Pruning category: B

Miss Bateman
Hybridizer: Noble, 1869

The flowers here are not large for an early-flowerer but very numerous, all of them coming in one rush. An attractively shaped flower, 5in (12cm) across, the eight ovate sepals are flat, overlapping for two-thirds of their length, with finely tapered tips. The central rib down the back of each sepal has a green stripe, appearing on the translucent white upper surface as a cream bar; occasionally the green bar will show on the upper face, when it appears even more attractive. The filaments are white, shading to pink at the anthers, which are themselves chocolate-red, providing a fine contrast. The leaves are ternate on a fairly compact grower, bushing out well to the sides.

Flowers: May–June
Height: 6ft (1.8m)
Pruning category: B

Miss Crawshay

Hybridizer: Jackman, 1873

There is a dearth of clear pink among clematis and at the same time a preponderance of mauve-pink varieties. This is one of those, on the pale pink side of mauve. The eight round-ended sepals are superimposed with one or two layers of smaller rounded sepals, rather casually disposed, the 6in (15cm) blooms having a silky texture. The filaments are white with pale beige anthers. The leaves are ternate. A moderate grower, which is pleasant, if not outstanding.

Flowers: June, and August
Height: 6ft (1.8m)
Pruning category: B

Moonlight

Hybridizer: unknown

Although there are no deep yellow large-flowered clematis, two hybrids do show enough colour to be classed as yellow. This, with its appropriate name, inclines much more to yellow than 'Wada's Primrose' (see page 83).

Opposite: 'Miss Crawshay'

'Moonlight'

The flowers, 5–6in (12–15cm) across, have a charming informal shape resembling shallow cups. The eight sepals (occasionally there are extra ones) are long and obovate, with a cuspidate apex. They first open a light green-yellow, changing to cream-yellow with a primrose central bar, which, on the reverse, is a green stripe. In some seasons there may be a shaded maroon stain towards the ends of the sepals; the stamens are large and creamy-yellow. The flower buds are distinctive in that they are twisted, with the sepal points bypassing one another like the top of a wigwam, instead of being closed together; they are quite hairy. The ternate leaves are grey-green, curled or wavy.

Although it is rather slow to establish itself and not a vigorous plant, who could deny a home to such a serene beauty? It is essential, however, to choose a shady site; such a delicate complexion fades to nothing in the sun.

Flowers: May–June
Height: 5ft (1.5m)
Pruning category: B

Mrs Cholmondeley
Hybridizer: Noble, 1873

If any of the large-flowered hybrids can be described as almost fool-proof, it must be this one. It is a very amenable plant; if pruned as instructed it will start flowering in late spring for Group B, and carry on with vigorous growth, until stopped by frost. For a more restrained plant, prune as for Group C when flowering will commence in July and continue until autumn.

Each flower consists of six, sometimes seven, obovate sepals, widely spaced and tapering sharply to the base, being slightly convex along their length. Light lavender-blue in colour, paler along the midribs and distinguished by a network of veins in a darker shade, it combines happily with many other climbers. The filaments are white, and the anthers are brown. Leaflets are usually in threes, but some are in fives.

Flowers: May–October
Height: 20ft (6m)
Pruning category: B/C

Opposite: 'Mrs Cholmondeley'

'Mrs George Jackman'

Mrs George Jackman
Hybridizer: Jackman, 1873

'Mrs George Jackman' is very similar to 'Marie Boisselot' (see page 61), but it tends to be rather creamy along the midribs and it does not achieve quite the same size, although this, too, is a large flower. The main difference, though, lies in the stamens which form a dome, the white filaments tipped with pale beige anthers. A good performer, it is not quite as vigorous as 'Marie Boisselot'.

Flowers: May-June, and September
Height: 8ft (2.4m)
Pruning category: B

Mrs James Mason
Hybridizer: Fretwell, 1984

Since its introduction, 'Mrs James Mason' has become the best-selling plant at the nursery in its flowering season. The flowers are large, 7in (28cm) across, the eight sepals wide and overlapping but not lying flat, as each sepal is dished, almost boat-shaped along its length, the edges attractively waved and frilled. The colour is a vibrant violet-blue, with a central velvet dark red bar. The first flowers of the season from old wood are surmounted by numerous shorter inner rows of lilac sepals, which tend to obscure the brightly coloured guard sepals. My preference is for the quite prolific display of later, single flowers. The very large boss of rich cream stamens is a most noticeable feature. The leaves are solitary and ternate.

A vigorous grower and free flowering, it is a plant that shows if it is being underfed; the flowers will then take on a decidedly paler complexion. This may also happen in the first year until the plant has settled down. The parentage is 'Vyvyan Pennell' × 'Dr Ruppel'.

Flowers: May–June, and September
Height: 6–10ft (1.8–3m)
Pruning category: B

Mrs N. Thompson
Hybridizer: Pennell, 1961

An eye-catching variety to which the spectator is irresistibly drawn. The deep violet-purple sepals have bright red bars along the centre; the newly opened flower has a rich velvet sheen, but this fades to as matt a surface as it started out velvet. The 5in (12cm) flowers have four, five or six sepals, irregularly waved, lying in a rather disorientated way. The stamens are small, forming no contrast, and the filaments are pink, with dark red anthers. Although it flowers well enough, it has, regrettably, a rather weak constitution.

Flowers: May–June, and September
Height: up to 4ft (1.2m)
Pruning category: B

Mrs P. B. Truax
Hybridizer: unknown

This is exceptional among the large-flowered hybrids, quite different from the usual flat, plate-like or star-shaped types. At the apex the sepals, eight in number, are rounded and wide although not touching, but halfway down they quickly taper to a narrow base. The tips also reflex as if the narrow base cannot quite support the weight; the gappy open shape thus formed is a refreshing variation on a familiar theme. There is a slight green flush in the midrib and, although the pale blue colour is not unique, it has the most silky-textured sepals that you could wish to see, irresistible to the touch. Even the deep cream stamens have a silky look about them. The leaves are ternate and not overpowering. Occasionally, a few flowers appear in the autumn, but the main display is in early summer. A moderate grower.

Flowers: May–June
Height: up to 6ft (1.8m)
Pruning category: B

Mrs Spencer Castle
Hybridizer: unknown

It may seem rather tedious to repeat the description 'mauve-pink', but that is the colour; subtle differences, apparent when the flower is seen, are not always easy to convey in words. This is probably the pinkest of the mauve-pink range, each of the six sepals tapering to long points and barely overlapping at the base. From the base of each sepal a rosy-pink flush radiates along the midrib, gradually merging into the pale pink in a most appealing way. The filaments are lilac-pink, the anthers cream. The ternate leaves are not over abundant.

The first flowers of the season often have extra sepals, creating a semi-double bloom, but they are rather unevenly distributed and I think the single flowers are preferable. A moderate grower, the second flower display is exceptionally good. I have always had a soft spot for this variety, which certainly numbers in my top 10.

Flowers: May–June, and August–September
Height: 6ft (1.8m)
Pruning category: B

Nelly Moser
Hybridizer: Moser, 1897

This is almost too well-known to need description, except that sheer familiarity with the name leads to it being ascribed to any remotely similar clematis. Its popularity is based on the long-established virtue of vigour and show-stopping display. The eight sepals are wide and overlapping, the rounded tips adding to the overall circular effect, pale rosy-mauve in colour with wide central carmine bars, and the sepals taper inwards at the base, leaving a perforated pattern around the centre. The stamens are large and well shaped, the white filaments shading to pink at the dark maroon anthers. The leaves are ternate.

The large, flat blooms, 8in (20cm) across, look you straight in the eye and can be so numerous as to almost obscure the foliage. The only disadvantage is that in a sunny position the colouring fades so quickly that within a matter of days all that is left is an unattractive dirty-white. Vigorous indeed, spreading almost as wide as it grows tall, I well remember seeing growing across the front of an old farmhouse a plant that must have

Opposite above: 'Mrs James Mason'; opposite below: 'Mrs N. Thompson'

Opposite above: 'Mrs P.B. Truax'; opposite below: 'Nelly Moser'
'Mrs Spencer Castle'

measured about 15ft (4.5m) high with a spread of some 20ft (6m).

Flowers: May–June, and September
Height: 8–10ft (2.4–3m)
Pruning category: B

Niobe
Hybridizer: Noll, 1975

This is one of those awkward varieties that sits uncomfortably astride the pruning fence.

You can prune this hard if you wish, in which case it will put on a good show from young growth in the autumn. The alternative, however, is to prune lightly, when it will start to flower in early summer and carry on virtually non-stop until the autumn. As it is not a tall-growing variety, I always opt for the latter method. The six sepals taper to sharp points, scarcely overlapping the base and sweeping upwards and outwards to create a cup-shaped star. The colour on opening is an extremely dark, almost black, ruby-red, which changes to a bright ruby. The cream stamens form a fine contrast. The ternate leaves are sharply tapering and rather neat. A moderate grower and although never a mass of bloom, it is rarely without some flowers throughout the season. These start the early season at around 6in (15cm); the later ones are about 4in (10cm).

Flowers: June–September
Height: 8ft (2.4m)
Pruning category: B/C

Perle d'Azur
Hybridizer: Morel, c.1885

This is without a doubt one of the most popular clematis ever raised. Of true C. × jackmanii persuasion, its flowers come in one huge mass, starting in midsummer and keeping this unbroken blanket of colour into the autumn. The sepals, four, five or six, are rounded, sometimes overlapping, often with gaps, and corrugated along the midribs with the tips reflexed in a very distinctive way. The 5in (12cm) wide flowers are not individually inspiring, but such is the density of bloom, that this seems a mere triviality. Always described as sky-blue, which, of course, it is not, the flowers have a definite rosy flush at the base of the midribs, although they give the impression of being a clear, light blue. The small stamens are light green. The leaves, ternate and in fives, are plentiful but almost obscured by the flowers.

An extremely good and vigorous plant, it is the only one of the C. × jackmanii group in this colour. Newly planted young plants seem prone to wilt, although they invariably grow away as strong as ever after this initial setback.

Flowers: June–September
Height: 10–15ft (3–4.5m)
Pruning category: C

Peveril Pearl
Hybridizer: Fretwell, 1979

Nobody could have failed to realize that I have a definite attachment to the paler shades although this does not debar appreciation of the deeper tones. Here, the pale lilac-pink of the sepals has a deeper flush along the midribs, with an overall opaque, pearl-like lustre. The eight sepals taper to rounded tips and overlap for half their length, making an attractive outline. The stamens are large and well-formed, and the white filaments are tipped with lilac-beige anthers. The early flowers are large, 8in (20cm) across, the later ones being somewhat smaller.

A moderately strong grower, 'Peveril Pearl' flowers very well, with solitary and ternate foliage. Although none of the pale shades are suitable for sunny spots where they fade to nothing all too quickly, they have the compensating property of illuminating dark corners or north walls and, in the early evening light, appear to take on a strange luminosity.

Flowers: May–June, and September
Height: 6ft (1.8m)
Pruning category: B

Pink Fantasy
Hybridizer: unknown

This is about as near to a true pink flower as exists among the autumn-flowering clematis. It is a pretty shell-pink, with a deeper bright pink bar along the centre of each of the six sepals, which are broad, although short, and the flower is only about 6in (15cm) wide. The pink bar varies in size and density of colour, not only from flower to flower but also on different sepals in the same flower, and some of the sepals twist and curl in a most informal way. The stamens are small, with reddish-beige anthers. Leaves are ternate, narrow and tapering. The pink colouring does fade in the bright sun to mauve-pink, so it is wise to consider this when planting. Although it is not a very strong or vigorous variety, it is free flowering.

Flowers: July–September
Height: 6ft (1.8m)
Pruning category: C

Opposite above: 'Niobe'; opposite below: 'Perle d'Azur'

'Proteus'

Proteus
Hybridizer: Noble, 1876

Mauve-pink again, but definitely on the mauve side, with a rather dim rosy-lilac colour apparent on close inspection, appearing more pink from a distance. The 6in (15cm) wide, early flowers are packed with sepals, rather in the manner of a double paeony. The later flowers, coming from the current season's growth, are in complete contrast, each with six narrow sepals, tapering to fine points. The stamens are creamy. The foliage is ternate and stays within bounds. It can be slow to get started, but is a moderately good grower.

Flowers: June, and September
Height: 6ft (1.8m)
Pruning category: B

feature that does not appear until the plant has become established in the garden is the rosy-pink shading that suffuses the midribs.

It is the stamens, however, that are such a feature of this variety and worthy of special note: the filaments are red, with bright golden-yellow anthers. They do not stand erect in the normal way, but swirl rather as if brushed deliberately into this shape. The leaves are ternate and sharply tapered. A plant of good constitution, vigorous though not tall, and very free flowering.

Flowers: May–June, and September
Height: 8ft (2.4m)
Pruning category: B

Richard Pennell
Hybridizer: Pennell, 1974

Distinguished by very large flowers, 8in (20cm) across, of a pleasant rosy-purple shade, paling towards the central ribs. The eight sepals are wide and overlapping and taper to blunt tips, the edges slightly undulating. A

Opposite: 'Peveril Pearl'

Rouge Cardinal
Hybridizer: unknown

A fairly new introduction from France, this variety is deep crimson in colour, with lighter red highlights. The rich velvet texture does not prevent it from fading to the usual beetroot-red. The flowers are not large, 4in (10cm); this would be irrelevant if the plant was free-flowering – unfortunately it is not. The six sepals are very blunt-ended, barely overlapping, consequently

forming a rounded flower. The stamens are small, with beige anthers. The leaves are ternate.

Flowers: July–September
Heighty: 6ft (1.8m)
Pruning category: C

Scartho Gem

Hybridizer: Pennell, 1973

The parentage of this variety, 'Lincoln Star' × 'Mrs N. Thompson', seems an odd choice to pair together considering the rather weak constitution of both parents. This trait has, unfortunately, been handed down to the offspring, which is a pity because it is a pleasing clematis and as a smaller grower could have many uses – not every position needs a 'Mrs Cholmondeley' or a 'King Edward VII'. Assuming that a variety has enough bonus points to counter some deficiency, it is worthy of a position.

This is the brightest pink among the large-flowered hybrids. The eight sepals are a true bright cochineal-pink, with a lighter pink area round the edge, wide and overlapping with waved edges. The stamens are large, with white filaments and pink-red anthers. The flowers, at 6in (15cm) across, keep their colour quite well in the sun and are very freely produced, so much so that there is little left to make new growth. The small leaves are ternate. It is rather slow to get started.

Flowers: May–June, and September
Height: 6ft (1.8m)
Pruning category: B

Sealand Gem

Hybridizer: Bees, c.1950

'Sealand Gem' is rarely seen today although it is a very good grower. The pale lavender-blue sepals have dull carmine bars, overlapping and rounded at the tips. The filaments are white, the anthers reddish. Foliage is ternate. In essence, it is a bluer-toned 'Nelly Moser', the growth as vigorous and the flowers just as large, to 8in (20cm), unfortunately with the same propensity to fade.

Flowers: May–June, and September
Height: 10ft (3m)
Pruning category: B

Opposite above: 'Richard Pennell'; opposite below: 'Rouge Cardinal'

Star of India

Hybridizer: Cripps, 1867

This has the true C. × *jackmanii* persuasion although the flower is a more attractive shape, the four, five or six sepals, wide at the apex, overlapping. The newly opened flower is wholly red-plum in colour, although this quickly changes to violet-purple, with a softly-merging central band of plum purple-red. A lively flower, which catches the eye more than C. × *jackmanii*, the stamens are small, with greenish filaments and brown anthers. The well-shaped flowers appear larger at 5in (12cm), than C. × *jackmanii* but are not produced in the same prodigious mass, although they are still plentiful. The leaves are ternate, and some of the upper ones have five leaflets, large and very dark green. It grows reasonably well, although not as strongly as C. × *jackmanii*.

Flowers: Late June–September
Height: 12ft (3.6m)
Pruning category: C

Susan Allsop

Hybridizer: Pennell, 1973

This has attractively formed flowers, eight dull blue-purple guard sepals, with a dim magenta flush along the midribs, overlapping and tapering to points. The inner narrow sepals of similar colour are arranged in tightly packed, neat symmetrical layers, finished with a central eye of cream stamens. Well-formed single flowers follow in the autumn; the sepals are quite stiff and do not bruise so easily in the wind. It flowers freely, and is also a vigorous grower, but the matt finish to the flowers detracts from it. A recent introduction called 'Royalty' is so similar to this variety that, when first seen, it could be assumed to be exactly the same.

Flowers: May–June, and September
Height: 8ft (2.4m)
Pruning category: B

The President

Hybridizer: Noble, 1876

A variety that can still hold its own after more than 100 years, demonstrated by the fact that it has remained popular in the nursery and garden-centre trade. A bold, handsome flower, fully 7in (18cm) across, the large, slightly cupped blooms have eight overlapping sepals tapering to points with lightly undulating edges, exposing the silvery undersides. The purple-blue colour is deep but lacks solidity, the stamens large and striking, and the filaments white with reddish-purple anthers.

The tapered, ternate leaves are tinged bronze in the young foliage.

Few clematis can claim to be almost perpetually flowering, and one of the reasons for this variety's perennial popularity is its claim to be just that. It is vigorous and easy to grow.

Flowers: May–September
Height: 6–10ft (1.8–3m)
Pruning category: B

Veronica's Choice
Hybridizer: Pennell, 1973

Many of the older double clematis had weak constitutions, and possibly for that reason they have long since passed into oblivion. Today's gardeners are better served, and it is with strong-growing, amenable varieties such as this that public confidence in double-flowered clematis is being restored. This is a very pretty, frilly-looking flower, with strong, crisp sepals, 6in (15cm) wide.

The eight outer guard sepals are wide with undulating edges, the tips being blunt but with a fine apical point. The pale lavender ground is shaded and streaked with rosy-lilac. The next four or five inner rows of quite wide sepals are very pale lavender lightly shaded in a deeper tone, and smaller, narrower sepals in the same shade continue to the centre, almost covering the creamy stamens. Single flowers follow in the autumn. The ternate foliage is rather large but not over-powering. It is a strong-growing variety, and the parentage is given as 'Vyvyan Pennell' × 'Percy Lake'.

Flowers: May–June, and September
Height: 6–8ft (1.8–2.4m)
Pruning category: B

Victoria
Hybridizer: Cripps, 1870

A *C. × jackmanii* type, displaying the pendent flower buds and nodding flowers so distinctive of this group, a characteristic they obtain from their direct viticella descent. The four, five or six sepals are widest across the middle, tapering to blunt tips, scarcely overlapping and lying not quite flat, the overall shape being slightly reflex.

In a newly opened flower the colour is rosy-purple, rosy along the midrib, but fading to a soft heliotrope. The plant looks most attractive when displaying flowers through varying degrees of colour change. The colour is

'Veronica's Choice'

concentrated along the three central ribs and the veins, which are sunken, creating a rather textured surface. Stamens are small, with greenish-white filaments, and the anthers are pale beige. Leaflets are borne in fives and are rather large. The 5–6in (12–15cm) flowers are as profuse as those of *C. × jackmanii,* and the growth is equally vigorous.

Flowers: June–September
Height: 8–10ft (2.4–3m)
Pruning category: C

Ville de Lyon
Hybridizer: Morel, 1899

Francisque Morel, who raised this variety, was, to my mind, the finest hybridizer of all. George Jackman produced far more, but the majority of these were mid-season hybrids, which can be turned out by the thousand. Not so with Morel, who trod a more difficult route to fame.

Morel gave the parentage for this plant as *C. coccinea* (which was the old name for *C. texensis*) as the pollen parent and 'Vivian Morel'. He also produced other texensis hybrids, which relate very much to the typical elongated tulip-shape. My own work with texensis has produced varying shapes, but never anything near the flattened form of the large-flowered hybrids. It seems to me more likely that Morel was referring to a texensis F_1 hybrid in the raising of 'Ville de Lyon'. This is another of the half dozen ubiquitous varieties stocked by most garden centres for its undeniable reputation for vigour.

The six sepals are wide, obovate and very blunt at the tips, with the margins and tips reflexed. A carmine band round the edge merges into a lighter inner area; as the flower fades, the inner area changes to a strange murky mauve. The stamens are large for a late-flowering variety, if rather spidery, the creamy colour contrasting well with the sepals. Leaflets are in threes and fives, the basal ones prematurely turning brown as far up as 3ft (90cm). This is unavoidable, although it will start earlier in the season if there has been any shortage of water or nutrients. A vigorous grower if room permits, it can be lightly pruned, with consequent earlier blooms; hard pruning will restrict it to about 10ft (3m) or so. Whichever method you choose, there will hardly be a week without flower, so freely are these produced over a long period.

Flowers: May–September
Height: 10–30ft (3–9m) dependent on pruning
Pruning category: B/C

'Victoria'

Opposite: 'Ville de Lyon'

Vyvyan Pennell
Hybridizer: Pennell, 1959

Although new compared with most other double-flowering cultivars, this is the best known, not only because it is a stronger grower than most, but also because it is named after the wife of its raiser, who initiated the revival of interest in clematis during the 1950s.

It produces two good flower displays, with equal abandon covering the stems from near the base to the outermost edges. This is just as well, for it is a colouring that does not mix easily.

The first flowers, measuring 6–7in (15–17cm) across and arising from the previous year's growth, are fully double, dome-shaped rosettes of lavender-blue, shaded with a strange reddish-brown and sitting on eight violet guard sepals. This unusual colouring appeals to many, but my preference is for the quite generous later crop of single flowers, from the current year's growth; they are a luminous silver-violet. The stamens are cream. The leaves are ternate and large. It is strong growing, bushing well outwards to a spread equalling the height.

Flowers: May–June, and September
Height: 6–7ft (1.8–2.1m)
Pruning category: B

Wada's Primrose
Hybridizer: unknown

As if designed to cause headaches among gardeners, both this and the near-similar 'Moonlight' (see page 67) were originally sold under the name 'Yellow Queen'.

The eight sepals are obovate, tapering to points and lying flatter than in 'Moonlight', they also differ in overlapping halfway from the base. The yellow colour is paler, more of a soft cream, with the central stripe creamy-primrose; the stamens are cream. The ternate leaflets are heart-shaped, and smaller and more numerous than those of 'Moonlight'.

'Wada's Primrose' is a much more vigorous plant than 'Moonlight', but the numerous stems are rather thin, and it is a leafy and bushy plant. It is rather a matter of choosing between a more difficult, but to me, more attractive 'Moonlight' and an easier, paler version in 'Wada's Primrose'. The early flowering season is identical, with anything in the autumn to be looked upon as a bonus.

Flowers: May–June
Height: 6ft (1.8m)

'Vyvyan Pennell'

Walter Pennell

Hybridizer: Pennell, 1974

Unusual colours do not at all lend themselves to the written word. Always described in catalogues as deep pink, this over-simplification does nothing to convey the true likeness.

The guard sepals, usually six (occasionally there are seven or eight), are rounded at the ends, cuspidate, finishing with a small point, and with gaps in between. Down the centre of each runs a dark carmine bar, and on either side is a light area of slaty mauve-pink; this darkens into a deeper mauve-pink around the edges, the extreme outer edges being etched with a fine carmine line. Surmounting the guard sepals are 30–40 small, wavy-edged sepals, lilac-grey with mauve-pink shadings. The stamens are pale cream, and the leaves are ternate. A reasonably vigorous grower, 'Walter Pennell' has a good repeat flowering of single blooms in the autumn.

Flowers: May–June, and September
Height: 8ft (2.4m)
Pruning category: B

W. E. Gladstone

Hybridizer: Noble, 1881

Surely it is an advantage that large-flowered varieties like this one do not bloom with the massed freedom of some of the earlier flowering kinds; a purity of outline can be appreciated far more if it is uncluttered by the shoulder-to-shoulder aggressiveness of some. Easily competing in the large flower stakes, this variety is capable of producing 10in (25cm) yet perfectly formed flowers, the seven sepals wide and overlapping, tapering to points, flat with a slight reflexing at the outer edges. They are a clear lavender with a silky texture and a conspicuous boss of very large stamens, white filaments and maroon anthers. The ternate leaves are large, each leaflet reaching 6in (15cm) long by 4in (10cm) wide, although they are not numerous as the nodes are set at intervals of 10–15in (25–38cm).

With light pruning, flowering will start in June and carry on spasmodically until the autumn; hard pruning means a later start, the young growth beginning in July and flowering progressively as the growth extends. The latter pruning method may be enforced as, in common with a few other varieties, 'W. E. Gladstone' will succomb to a hard winter. All top growth down to ground level can be killed off, but it will usually regrow from the base with renewed vigour. It never has a multiplicity of shoots, and it is ideal when climbing through a shrub or through a climbing rose such as 'Gloire de Dijon'.

Flowers: June–September
Height: 12ft (3.6m)
Pruning category: B/C

William Kennett

Hybridizer: unknown, 1875

This has been consistently popular since its introduction and is, for the first-time grower of these exquisite climbers, one of the most rewarding. Normally there are eight sepals, although flowers on the young wood often have only six or seven. The sepals are very wide, tapering to short points and firmly overlapping, with strongly undulating margins. The rich lavender-blue is more pronounced along the nerves and veins, and a dull reddish flush radiates from the centre along each rib, although this gradually fades. The 7in (18cm) flowers are handsome and striking, with their large dark maroon anthers and white filaments. The large, heart-shaped leaves are solitary.

This is one of the most trouble-free plants, vigorous and with a long flowering season. If space is limited, it can be pruned hard back in the spring as flowering from the current season's growth is excellent.

Flowers: May–September
Height: 10–20ft (3–6m)
Pruning category: B

SPECIES AND SMALL-FLOWERED HYBRIDS

C. addisonii

Country of origin: USA (southwest Virginia)

A most delightful herbaceous perennial. Each stem ter-
minates in a solitary flower; side-shoots, also with a
terminal flower, grow out from the final node. The
pitcher-shaped, nodding flowers, 1in (25mm) long and
$\frac{3}{4}$in (18mm) wide at the base, narrowing towards the
mouth, are borne on long stalks and are typical of the
viornae group (see *C. viorna*, page 142). The four sepals
are thick and fleshy, narrowly-ovate and very reflexed at
the tips so as to display the clear cream interior to better
effect. The exterior colour is a rich rosy-purple, this colour being carried partially into the flower stem. The
stamens, which are more or less hidden inside the flower,
are cream. The very distinctive leaves are wide, heart-
shaped, solitary and borne on leaf stalks so short as to
give the appearance almost of one perfoliate leaf, smooth
and glaucous. Never a mass of flower, but lively, this
little plant is hardy if given a warm border that does not
retain water in the winter.

Flowers: June–July
Height: 12–15in (30–38cm)
Pruning category: C

C. aethusifolia

Country of origin: China, 1855

It must have amused others besides myself that this
clematis was shown on a television programme as having been just brought back from China and still to be
identified. Never very common, it has been one of my
favourites for many years; it is unlikely that it will ever
become popular or numerous for this lovely plant is
extremely difficult to propagate, the cuttings being
slow and seemingly unwilling to take.

The stems are very slender with 8in (20cm) leaves
divided into three, five and seven leaflets which are
further divided into irregular lobes, creating the pret-
tiest lace-like foliage that is known among clematis. The
small, bell-shaped flowers, $\frac{1}{2}$in (12mm) long, have four
strongly ribbed sepals with recurved tips; they are
borne in threes or fives from every node along the final
2–3ft (60–90cm) of stem. They are a pale primrose shade
and have creamy-white stamens.

Flowers: July–September
Height: 5–7ft (1.5–2m)
Pruning category: C

Pages 86–7: *C. × jouiniana* 'Praecox';

Below: *C. addisonii*

C. afoliata

Country of origin: New Zealand, 1871

So unusual is this plant that it always evokes if not admiration, then curiosity. Commonly called the rush-stemmed clematis, it is, indeed, similar to the hard rush commonly found in damp meadows, and the name gives some indication of the appearance of this rather strange climber.

The stems have numerous side branches which themselves are branched, deep green, smooth and wiry, forming a large net of intertwining stems. The leaves are usually reduced to only the leaf stalks which act like tendrils. Some leaves are present, noticeably on young plants and consist of three triangular-shaped leaflets about $\frac{1}{4}$in (6mm) across. The flowers are pale yellow with a greenish tinge, $\frac{1}{2}$–$\frac{3}{4}$in (12–18mm) across, with a silky texture, the four narrow sepals forming a slightly reflexed star. As with all the 10 species native to New Zealand, this is dioecious, the males bearing the larger, more distinctly yellow flowers, with cream stamens.

Although it can be grown against a wall, its rather untidy habit is more suited to scrambling on the ground among other shrubs, as long as a warm and sheltered position is available. It is not hardy in cold districts, but plants in the more favoured areas have survived for many years.

Flowers: May
Dimensions: 6 × 6ft (1.8 × 1.8m)
Pruning category: A

C. alpina

Country of origin: Europe, north Asia, 1792

One of the hardiest, most easy-going plants imaginable, yet the flowers have a delicate charm that belies their tough constitution. Admirably suited to a north-facing, shady or cool position, this and its relatives are among the first clematis to start the year with a floral display.

The flowers, on long stalks, are produced singly, directly from the leaf axils of the previous year's growth, the four tapered sepals nodding like spiky bells $1\frac{1}{2}$in (4cm) long and wide, lavender-blue to purple-blue. Between the sepals and the stamens are a number of rows of staminodes (petal-like stamens) $\frac{1}{2}$in (12mm) long, whitish in colour. The seed heads are prominent, the grey, fluffy balls staying on until the winter. Occasional flowers are produced in the autumn; this seems to vary from year to year, and sometimes quite a respectable display can occur. The foliage is attractive, the leaves doubly ternate, each leaflet 1–2in (2.5–5cm) long and coarsely toothed.

C. afoliata

The true alpina is not always easily obtainable, the plants being offered at many garden centres at present being mongrels (with a certain amount of *C. macropetala* blood by their appearance), which are garden-worthy but not the genuine article.

Flowers: April–May
Height: 6–8ft (1.8–2.4m)
Pruning category: A

C. alpina 'Candy'
Hybridizer: Fretwell, 1986

There are various named seedlings from *C. alpina*. Usually the flowers are nodding, but in this variety they look you straight in the eye so that, instead of the outer sepal colour being the most conspicuous, it is the inner colour that takes the stage. Although similar in size to *C. alpina*, the sepals are wider and more obliquely spread. The exterior is icing-sugar pink, the inside delicate pastel pink, this colour also shading the staminodes. The stamens are green.

Flowers: April–May
Height: 6–8ft (1.8–2.4m)
Pruning category: A

C. alpina 'Columbine'
Hybridizer: Markham, 1937

This is the nearest in form of the named varieties to the type species. The clear light blue sepals taper to finer points, and the staminodes are white. It is an elegantly poised little flower.

Flowers: April–May
Height: 6–8ft (1.8–2.4m)
Pruning category: A

C. alpina 'Jacqueline du Pré'
Hybridizer: Fretwell, 1985

This eye-catching variety is a more vigorous grower than the other alpinas and therefore requires rather more space to expand. The flowers, too, are larger, $2\frac{1}{2}$in (6cm) long, the sepals wider and tapering less sharply than *C. alpina*. The exterior colour is a warm rosy-mauve pink, the interior a pale powder-pink, around the outer edge of each sepals runs a narrow, conspicuous silver-pink margin, and the white staminodes are also flushed with pale pink.

Flowers: April–May
Height: 8–10ft (2.4–3m)
Pruning category: A

C. alpina 'Pamela Jackman'
Hybridizer: Jackman, 1960

A form with finely tapering sepals. The colour is a rich, deep purple-blue; the staminodes are white, although the outer ones are stained purple-blue.

Flowers: April–May
Height: 6–8ft (1.8–2.4m)
Pruning category: A

C. alpina 'Ruby'
Hybridizer: Markham, 1937

Typically alpina in form, the colour is not quite as ruby-red as the name suggests. The dusky mauve-red looks much brighter and livelier when bathed in spring sunlight; the staminodes are off-white shaded with dusky pink. There is no problem with growing this variety in a shady spot, but the colouring is less than satisfying there.

Flowers: April–May
Height: 6–8ft (1.8–2.4m)
Pruning category: A

C. alpina sibirica
Country of origin: northern Europe to Siberia, 1753

This natural variant is only sparsely distributed in the wild. It has regularly been described as creamy-white or yellow-white, and although there are undoubtedly creamy-white forms around, in its finer forms *C. alpina sibirica* is as pure as driven snow.

The general flower outline is typical alpina, although the four sepals are slightly narrower, tapering to sharper points and opening less widely. The inner staminodes are white with green stamens. The foliage is a distinctive light green, and the young growth pale yellow-green. The delicate beauty of the flower belies the tough character of the plant.

Some white-flowered forms have evolved from alpina; all have the dark green foliage typical of the type species and never seem to attain the grace of this wild species.

Flowers: April–May
Height: 6–8ft (1.8–2.4m)
Pruning category: A

C. alpina 'White Moth'

A double-flowering seedling of *C. alpina sibirica* but looking more akin to *C. macropetala* in form. The staminodes, however, are less sharply tapered and the flower more dumpy. The colour is, to put it kindly, less than white.

Opposite above: *C. alpina* 'Candy'; opposite below: *C. alpina* 'Columbine'

C. alpina 'Jacqueline du Pré'

Flowers: May
Height: 6ft (1.8m)
Pruning category: A

C. alpina 'Willy'

Hybridizer: unknown

This variety was introduced from Holland in the 1970s. The four sepals are narrow and taper to fine points; the very pale mauve-pink colour has a deeper cyclamen-pink blotch at the base of each sepal, and the staminodes are off-white.

A few other varieties came over from Holland at the same time; they were all rather dingy, in unattractive shades and seem to have disappeared from the scene.

Flowers: April–May
Height: 6–8ft (1.8–2.4m)
Pruning category: A

C. armandii

Country of origin: China, 1900

I am often asked if I have plants of *the* evergreen clematis. Notwithstanding that there are approximately 17 other evergreens, I know that this is invariably the one in question. It is also the hardiest, which undoubtedly adds to its popularity.

Even when not in flower, *C. armandii* attracts attention because of its large dark green, glossy leaves of a thick leathery texture that makes it appear almost indestructible. They are ternate, the central one larger, up to 6in (15cm) long. The flowers, 2in (5cm) across, are white or creamy-white, with usually four, sometimes up to six, blunt-ended sepals and with cream stamens; they are borne in large axillary clusters and have a strong vanilla scent, which is less obvious in inclement weather although still noticeable as temperatures rise.

This is a strong, vigorous grower; even with regular pruning it cannot be kept below 15ft (4.5m), and it is easily capable of doubling this height. It is wise to prune back to a main framework anyway, as the long side-growths pile one on each other, with mounds of slowly accumulating dead leaves underneath. It is important to do this as soon as flowering is over so as to allow time for the resultant new growth to ripen.

This species has proved much hardier than was once supposed. I grew the variety 'Apple Blossom' on the wall of a former home in the Peak District of Derbyshire at 1,000ft (300m) and only once in all the years it was there was it cut to ground level; the following spring, it

Opposite: *C. alpina sibirica*

romped away with renewed vigour. If necessary, quite old plants can be cut down to the base when they will quickly re-establish their former site.

Flowers: April–May
Height: 15–30ft (4.5–9m)
Pruning category: A

C. armandii 'Apple Blossom'

There are two named varieties of C. armandii, both more desirable than the species, both difficult to propagate and both, therefore, expensive (if you can find them). Therein lies a tale.

C. armandii itself is always in short supply, and large numbers are imported from Holland. The variability in the foliage among these plants suggests that a great many must be seedlings, and, as if to support this theory, there are plenty of armandiis around, with small, miserable flowers, and many plants are lost during the winter. It is the very variability of seedlings that makes them so undesirable; their flowers (or lack of them) and their hardiness are questionable. I wish it could be said that plants propagated in this country were guaranteed, but one still sees advertisements for seedlings of C. armandii 'Apple Blossom' claiming that 'all the flowers are good'. There is no possible way that such claims could be true given that the first flowers will occur long after a sale.

The true 'Apple Blossom' has six boat-shaped sepals, forming a saucer-shaped flower, 2–2½in (5–6cm) across; in colour it is a pale pink wash, with much deeper mauve-pink on the reverse. The young foliage is bronze, although this characteristic is not confined to this particular variety but is shared with other armandiis.

Flowers: April–May
Height: 15–30ft (4.5–9m)
Pruning category: A

C. armandii 'Snowdrift'

C. armandii 'Apple Blossom' received an Award of Merit from the Royal Horticultural Society in 1926 and has been with us for a long time. 'Snowdrift' was a Jackman introduction of a much later date; the plant described here, which I have grown for many years, is from that original stock. This is an outstanding armandii, the flowers a solid pure white, the six sepals wide and overlapping, with tips tapering to sharper points. The flower is flat and about 3in (8cm) across.

It greatly increases the selling potential if a plant can be tagged with an attractive-sounding name; it is highly probable that any plant you may just happen to come across will be no more than an ordinary armandii. It would be prudent to acquire a guarantee as to its authenticity for what is an unavoidably expensive plant, commensurate with its rarity.

Flowers: April–May
Height: 15–30ft (4.5–9m)
Pruning category: A

C. × aromatica
Country of origin: France, c.1857

Indeed, it is scented, not, as the name leads us to expect, with a welcoming fragrance, but rather with a scent that has to be sought after, although within 1ft (30cm) or so, the hawthorn-lemon scent is distinctly noticeable.

A semi-herbaceous perennial, C. × aromatica is quite tall, but without some support it will flop on to whatever happens to be nearby. The flowers are borne in large terminal panicles, the individual flowers being 1½in (4cm) wide, the four narrow sepals forming an open cruciform with slightly upturned tips. The strong violet-blue has a touch of reddish-purple on opening, with the large tuft of creamy-white stamens forming a most attractive contrast. The rather sparse leaves are non-clinging, solitary and ovate, but many have one or two lobes and some are even compound.

It has been described as a frail little plant. That has never been my experience, and I know of other plants which, like mine, regularly make clumps 3–4ft (1m) across. It is presumed to be a hybrid between C. integrifolia and C. flammula and it was originally named C. coerulea odorata.

Flowers: July–September
Height: 4–5ft (1–1.5m)
Pruning category: C

C. campaniflora
Country of origin: Portugal, 1820

This is a near relative of C. viticella with a similar growth habit, which, if hard pruned annually, can be kept within bounds. However, it is such a vigorous grower, especially if the chosen spot is really to its liking, that it will romp away to 25ft (7.5m), and it is wise to bear this in mind, although stems and foliage are as dainty as the flowers. These are elegant little nodding and open bells, the four sepals white with a violet wash, a more discernible colour on the outside, with the tips recurving in a most dainty manner. They are only 1¼in (3cm) but are

Opposite: C. armandii 'Apple Blossom'

borne in small clusters in profuse quantity. On young plants the flowers are often all white, and this has led to plants sometimes being offered as 'white forms' when in reality this is only a temporary stage. The stamens are green. The leaves, up to 6in (15cm) long, are pinnately divided into fives, sevens or nines, themselves composed of three leaflets. A pleasing, if not an eye-catching, plant.

Flowers: July–September
Height: approximately 15ft (4.5m)
Pruning category: C

C. chiisanensis

Country of origin: Korea

There are obvious close affinities here to the more commonly grown *C. tangutica*, the foliage especially is barely distinguishable from that species, bright sea-green and pinnate leaves, the leaflets irregularly and coarsely toothed.

The solitary flowers are pendent on very long stalks, up to 10in (25cm); each is composed of four sepals, 2–2½in (5–6cm) long, tapering sharply to fine points. The colour is a bright canary-yellow. One of the main attractions of *C. tangutica* is its large silvery seed-heads; they are considered large, but those of *C. chiisanensis* are enormous, the long, shaggy, silvery seed styles forming a rounded ball 4in (10cm) long and 3in (8cm) wide. This is a finer plant than *C. tangutica*, but almost inevitably it does have flaws. It is neither as tolerant of neglect as the better known *C. tangutica* nor as vigorous, although this is not to say that it is difficult, just more refined.

Flowers: July–September
Height: 10–15ft (3–4.5m)
Pruning category: C

C. chrysocoma

Country of origin: China, 1884

To a passer-by seeing a *C. chrysocoma* covering a wall or large tree, it would be taken for another montana, so obviously is it a very close relative of this well-known species. The long-stalked, 1½–2in (4–5cm) wide flowers are borne in axillary clusters of one to five flowers from the previous year's growth; each has four round-ended sepals almost as wide as they are long, overlapping and pale mauve-pink, deepening towards the edges; the stamens are creamy. Occasional flowers are borne throughout late summer but rarely enough to be called a

Opposite: *C.* × *aromatica*

display. The foliage is an obvious attraction, particularly the young leaves, which are reddish-bronze. The ternate leaflets have a broad, rounded outline, three-lobed, the central one larger, and both surfaces, the stems and the flower buds are covered in short golden hairs.

I have always called this a more refined montana; it is less rampant, although still very vigorous, and is perhaps better if grown along a wall or some other horizontal feature where the young growth can be fully appreciated. The flowers also look less pink if they are seen at the extremities of some 20ft (6m) tree. When Bean described the species in the first edition of *Trees and Shrubs Hardy in the British Isles* (1914), he gave it as a semi-woody shrub to 6–8ft (1.8–2.4m). It is still listed as such in the revised edition and still often slavishly, but erroneously, copied. The famous old firm of Veitch listed the species soon after its introduction and their description fits exactly the plant that we are familiar with today. Seedlings of chrysocoma do, indeed, stay bushy for some time before deciding to head skywards; it can only be assumed that the plant was originally described while still in a juvenile state.

Flowers: May–June
Height: 20ft (6m)
Pruning category: A

C. cirrhosa

Country of origin: southern Europe, 1596

Although this evergreen species will start flowering in November and carry a sizeable crop during any mild spell until February, an exceptionally hard winter will kill not only flower buds but also most of the foliage. Away from milder parts of the country it requires the protection of a warm wall; in more southerly areas a north-facing position is quite suitable.

The small, shiny leaves are simple, three-lobed, some cut so deeply as to appear as leaflets, and coarsely toothed. The flowers, 1½–2in (4–5cm) across, open green-white, changing to creamy-white. There are four sepals in an inverted saucer-shape, rough textured, nodding, with greenish stamens. They are produced in pairs from the axils on short stalks.

Although not as vigorous as the variety *balearica*, it far outstrips the few feet it was given by Bean. I recently acquired a plant under the name of *C. cirrhosa* 'Wisley Variety', which some enterprising nursery was offering for a rather large sum. As this does not differ one jot from the type species, I enquired after its special features. 'It does not have any red spots,' was the reply.

Flowers: Winter
Height: 15ft (4.5m)
Pruning category: A

C. cirrhosa var. *balearica*
Country of origin: Balearic Isles, 1783

This is a more popular plant than the type species, but whether it is more attractive depends on how you view a plant. The flowers, which are of similar size, have the same open, nodding saucers slightly upturned at the tips, but the colour is more yellow-white, and the insides are speckled with little longitudinal spots of reddish-maroon; otherwise they have the same textured surface, with green bracts behind the flower head.

The foliage is more finely divided than that of *C. cirrhosa*, the simple leaves cleft into three parts and these again are usually three-lobed, serrated and toothed. The evergreen foliage turns bronze-green in the winter months. I have another form in which the foliage is even more fern-like, the leaves deeply and unevenly cut into very fine divisions.

It is a stronger grower than *C. cirrhosa*; I know of several large specimens, one covering the entire gable end of a house and looking a picture in February when covered in flower. It is also hardier; another specimen grows through a deciduous tree near the edge of Dartmoor, in Devon, England, yet still manages to flower.

C. cirrhosa var. *balearica*

Opposite: *C. columbiana*

Flowers: Winter
Height: 15–25ft (4.5–7.5m)
Pruning category: A

C. columbiana
Country of origin: western USA, 1889

This and its close relative, *C. verticillaris*, are the American equivalents of the European *C. alpina*. There are, however, major differences in flower, leaf and cultivation.

The flower has the same nodding habit as *C. alpina*, but the four sepals are wider, tapering to points and not so widespread, giving the flower a more lax appearance. The colour is violet-blue to blue, in some forms as clear a blue as I have met among the clematis. This colour is not solid but has a beautiful translucent quality, the sepals having the texture of ricepaper lanterns and the veins showing through in a deeper colour.

The foliage, too, is distinctive, being ternate, unlike the biternate leaves of the alpinas; the leaflets are smooth, with occasional blunt teeth as opposed to the regular serrations of alpina. It is a rare plant in cultivation

because, although hardy, it is rather difficult and challenging to grow.

Flowers: May
Height: 5–8ft (1.5–2.4m)
Pruning category: A

C. connata
Country of origin: Tibet, Himalayas, western China, 1885

A rather strong-growing species with stout stems and large pale green, slightly hairy leaves up to 8in (20cm) long. They are divided into three to five heart-shaped leaflets, occasionally lobed, tapering to a long point and coarsely toothed around the upper two-thirds. The leaf stalks clasp the stems, joining the opposite stalks.

Bean says C. connata resembles C. rehderiana, and this may be so in the leaf, but the flowers bear little, if any, likeness. They are pendulous bells, 1in (2.5cm) long and wide, borne in panicles of nine to 15 flowers. The four sepals in each flower, recurving at the tips, have a thick fleshy appearance, while the exterior has a crystalline texture, and the inside bears a fine down, which appears to sparkle in the light. Quite a strong primrose-yellow on the inside, paling considerably on the exterior. The flowers are numerous and exceptionally showy; the season, though, is short, over and gone in about four weeks.

Flowers: September–October
Height: 20ft (6m)
Pruning category: C

C. crispa
Country of origin: southeastern USA, 1726

When I started to grow clematis, very few of the American species were available and most were badly misnamed. As I re-introduced more of these forgotten plants I realized what exquisite gems we had been denying ourselves. Having grown most of the American species for some years now, I am sure that newcomers to these little-known species will be as entranced as I was.

This is a slender climber suitable for growing through the lightest shrub, with no inconvenience to its host. The 5in (13cm) leaf is divided into five to seven small and smooth, narrowly-ovate leaflets on 1in (2.5cm) stalks. The solitary flowers, on 3–4in (8–10cm) stalks, face outwards or nod slightly; they are 1in (2.5cm) wide and 1½–2in (4–5cm) long. The four sepals, which are lightly ribbed, converge and narrow to a point halfway down, then widen to about ½in (12mm), reflexing right back to touch the outside of the sepal, the edges being beautifully crimped. The colour ranges

from light blue to purple-blue; the centre is white and extends along the midrib forming a distinctive star. On the outside, the colour is pale lilac-blue. The stamens are cream. It flowers continuously over a long period, although generally rather sparsely. The stems die down to the ground in winter, and it is wise to protect the base from frost with a thick straw mulch.

Flowers: June–September
Height: 6–8ft (1.8–2.4m)
Pruning category: C

C. crispa 'Rosea'
Hybridizer: Fretwell, 1985

This is the result of a C. crispa × C. texensis hybrid crossed back with C. crispa. Foliage and flower shape are similar to C. crispa, although the flower itself is smaller and has a narrower outline. On the outside the colour is rose-pink, and the inside is deep pink-red with the same white star-shape from the centre. It may, like C. crispa, keep some old stems through the winter, but it is best pruned back to near ground level and given some winter protection.

Flowers: June–September
Height: 6–8ft (1.8–2.4m)
Pruning category: C

C. douglasii
Country of origin: western USA, 1889

This unusual small herbaceous perennial is far easier to grow than to acquire, and its slowness of propagation ensures that it will remain so into the foreseeable future. Growing to a height of 1–2ft (30–60cm), it is suitable for a fairly well-drained, sunny border or large rockery, and it is well worth the effort of covering the dormant crown in winter with straw or bracken. I have always found the small flowers tremendously appealing although, in common with some other species, it may look most unlike a familiar clematis plant. They are almost as round as they are long, having a rather rotund urn-shape and taper sharply to the mouth with just the tips of the four sepals recurving and showing the tight tuft of creamy stamens. The inside colour is a deep, warm rose-purple, the exterior slightly more lavender, appearing lighter than it really is due to a covering of silver-grey down, which also extends to the long flower-stalk.

The foliage is very neat, the 3–5in (8–13cm) leaves pinnately divided into five or seven narrow lanceolate

Opposite above: C. connata; opposite below: C. crispa

Opposite above: *C. crispa* 'Rosea'; opposite below: *C. douglasii*

leaflets of an attractive grey-green. Bean described this species as having bipinnate leaves, which I always understood to belong to *C. douglasii* var. 'Scottii', although I have received plants having both types of foliage under both names.

Flowers: May–June
Height: 1–2ft (30–60cm)
Pruning category: C

C. douglasii 'Rosea'

This is identical in every way except for the colour of the flowers. They are deep pink on the inside, paler, clear pink on the outside. It is even rarer in cultivation.

C. × durandii

Country of origin: France, 1870

This hybrid from a *C. integrifolia* × *C. jackmanii* cross is often described as a climber. It can, and often will, carry some old wood from the previous season, and if these stems are pruned back to 3 or 4ft (1–1.2m), as sometimes

recommended, a plant of 10ft (3m) is easily achieved. However, I would advise pruning right back to the ground every year, as even the 4–6ft (1.2–1.8m) of non-clinging growth it will produce is not the easiest to deal with. If possible, try to grow it through a shrub rather than over it in order to avoid the long, non-clinging shoots being damaged by strong winds.

While not always an easy plant to place, it is well worth the effort involved. The flowers, 4–5in (10–13cm) across, are of the most intense indigo-blue; the four, five or six sepals are irregularly waved, with three distinctive, deeply grooved ribs. The stamens form a yellow-white, barrel-shaped tuft. One of the easiest and most rewarding of garden plants, its non-stop flowering habit provides colour for three months of the year. The leaves are solitary, narrowly ovate, 4–6in (10–15cm) long and not at all intrusive.

It was, at one time, grown by the million in Holland for cut flowers and its easy and free-flowering disposition more than cancels out its awkward habit. It is sometimes listed as *C. integrifolia* 'Durandii', which is incorrect as it is a hybrid from that species.

Flowers: July–October
Height: 3–4ft (1–1.2m)
Pruning category: C

C. × durandii

Edward Pritchard
Hybridizer: Pritchard, 1950

This herbaceous perennial has an ephemeral quality, which only serves to heighten my surprise every spring when it reappears. The hardest winter has no effect on it, yet its yearly increase is painfully slow. Raised in Australia from a cross between *C. recta* and *C. heracleifolia* 'Davidiana', it throws up slender stems, the upper thirds of which bear sweetly scented panicles of dainty, narrow sepalled, cruciform flowers, 1½in (4cm) across, white but shading to mauve-pink and deepening towards the tips. The stamens are creamy-white. The leaves, 6–8in (15–20cm) long, are divided into five leaflets, irregularly lobed and generally coarsely serrated although some are smooth.

Attractive against a dark background, 'Edward Pritchard' needs rich soil and a sunny position.

Flowers: July–August
Height: 3–4ft (approximately 1m)
Pruning category: C

C. × eriostemon 'Hendersonii'

C. × eriostemon 'Hendersonii'
Hybridizer: Henderson, 1835

Crosses between *C. integrifolia* and *C. viticella* had been done on at least two occasions, apart from this hybrid, but Henderson's cross, a slender climb with unobtrusive foliage, flowering over a very long season, seems to be the sole survivor. The flowers are intermediate between the two, like a nodding, more bell-shaped viticella with the four sepals recurving just a little at the tips. The deep blue-purple is a little more rosy towards the centre, and the stamens form a small tuft of green-yellow. Leaves are simple and pinnate, with small lanceolate leaflets. It is an easy and rewarding plant.

Although it is sometimes described as being non-clinging, this is not so; enough leaves will be clasping ones to hoist it through or over its host.

There has always been some doubt as to the original parentage, and some years ago I decided to recreate the original cross. The resultant seedlings were too similar to the above to be worth releasing although they are possibly more attractive, being deep reddish-purple with bright yellow stamens.

Flowers: July–September
Height: 6–8ft (1.8–2.4m)
Pruning category: C

C. fargesii souliei

Country of origin: China, 1911

Quite a strong grower, this plant is equally suited to climb through a large shrub or small tree, or on a wall, if enough space is available. The pure white flowers have an attractive outline, the six obovate sepals, which are blunt at the tips, are crimped, giving them a ragged appearance. Compared with the overall size, the greenish-white stamens are large. The flowers are borne in threes, on axillary stalks, the central one opening first.

The leaves are large and abundant, 6–8in (15–20cm) long, and biternate, although some are three-lobed rather than divided; they are coarsely serrated. Young shoots are tinged with purple. If pruned hard in spring, flowering will start around the end of July. However, where plenty of space is available, say 20–25ft (6–7.5m), light pruning will permit flowering to commence in late May or early June and continue non-stop until early autumn. The flowers are never abundant, but there are enough to attract attention.

Flowers: May, or July–September
Height: 10–25ft (3–7.5m), depending on pruning
Pruning category: C

C. fargesii souliei

C. flammula

Country of origin: Europe, 1596

Although one of the earliest clematis to be introduced into Britain, this still ranks as one of the most popular of the climbing species. A most exuberant plant, its great billowing, foamy masses of flowers dispense a heavy hawthorn-like perfume all around the garden.

Individually the flowers are small, $1–1\frac{1}{2}$in (2.4–4cm) wide; the four narrow sepals are cruciform but fold back to the stalk after a few days. The white stamens are almost as prominent as the sepals. The flowers are borne in large terminal panicles, in a good clone, touching each other to form huge white clouds. The biternate leaves can be extremely variable in size and shape, the leaflets varying from rounded heart-shaped to lanceolate, but always neat and dark glossy green. In mild winters it is virtually evergreen. Unfortunately, cuttings are difficult to root, and most plants offered for sale will be from seed, with the inevitable result that some plants are excellent while others are without scent or have miserable greenish-white flowers about $\frac{1}{2}$in (12mm) across. Such was my experience many years ago when I purchased my first flammula.

Flowers: August–October
Height: 15–20ft (4.5–6m)
Pruning category: C

Opposite: *C. flammula*

C. flammula 'Ithaca'

In this variety from the island of the same name, the flowers are smaller than in the type species, but the sepals are wider, thereby giving a more solid effect. The main attraction, however, lies in the irregular silvery variegation that runs down the centre of each leaf.

C. florida
Country of origin: China, 1776

I feel extremely privileged to be able to describe this rare species from sight. Over the years, many writers have made reference to it, obviously with second-hand knowledge only as no European has seen a plant in living memory. I hope that from the illustration readers may share some of the excitement that I felt when the first flower bud opened, after a most traumatic journey from its homeland.

It is rare even in China, so I was delighted, in 1984, to receive from a friend the only plant collected from an area not open to foreigners. At its first flowering in May 1985 the white, 4in (10cm) flowers were appreciably larger than anticipated – Bean quoted $2\frac{1}{3}$–3in (5–8cm). The five or six tapered sepals overlap for half their length, with undulating edges; underneath each sepal a dull purple bar runs along the midrib. The stamens are most conspicuous, with the filaments white at the base, shaded with a gradually deepening purple towards the blackish-purple anthers. About halfway along the 6in (15cm) flower stem are two wide, heart-shaped bracts, sometimes with small lobes.

The 4in (10cm) leaves are ternate, with narrowly ovate leaflets, the central one being three-lobed, smooth with occasional fine serrations. A slender and spindly, rather open climber, it does not appear to flower continuously in the manner of its two better known varieties. It does seem to be less tender though, keeping a certain amount of wood through the winter.

Flowers: June–July
Height: 8ft (2.4m)
Pruning category: B

C. florida 'Alba Plena'
Country of origin: Japan

It would be impossible to date this plant as it was already an old cultivated variety in Japan, when it was introduced from there in the 19th century.

C. florida

The six guard sepals are to all intents similar to those in the type species except that the stripe on the reverse is green and the rest of the sepal greenish-white. In this completely sterile flower the stamens are reduced to staminodes or petal-like structures. They are packed into a tight central mass, gradually expanding into a green-white dome 3in (8cm) across; this central boss is so double that even after the guard sepals have fallen the staminodes continue to expand for another six weeks, the longest-lasting flower on a clematis that I know of. Flowers are produced from the young growth from early summer until well into autumn.

The plant needs a warm sheltered wall and even then the top growth is often killed to ground level in winter, with regrowth in spring. Like *C. florida* 'Sieboldii' (see below), it makes a fine conservatory plant. The leaves resemble that variety, some being biternate. Almost extinct a few years ago, *C. florida* 'Alba Plena' is now happily re-established.

Flowers: June–October
Height: 6–10ft (1.8–3m)
Pruning category: B

C. florida 'Sieboldii' (syn. *C. florida bicolor*)
Country of origin: Japan, 1837

The contrast of a large, lustrous purple centre set against creamy-white sepals has universal impact and charm. Tender to a degree, this climber needs, and deserves, a choice warm wall, but in favoured areas only. Elsewhere, a cold greenhouse or conservatory is the answer. *C. florida* 'Sieboldii' is ideally suited to container culture, and it has a remarkably long flowering period.

Leaves, up to 5in (13cm) long, are divided into three leaflets, the bottom pair sometimes again divided into three, sharply pointed and slightly toothed or lobed. Flowers are produced progressively on the terminal 3ft (1m) of new growth and borne on 6in (15cm) long stalks with a distinctive pair of leaf-like bracts about the middle. The five or six sepals are greenish-white changing to creamy-white; the anthers are transformed into narrow, petal-like structures forming a central dome. This starts as a light greeny-purple, changing to deep purple, and remains for four or five days after the sepals have fallen.

Flowers: June–September
Height: 6–10ft (1.8–3m)
Pruning category: B/C

C. forsteri
Country of origin: New Zealand, 1853

A dioecious evergreen, growing strongly into a mass of tangled stems. The leaves are ternate, with 1–2in (2.5–5cm) long leaflets lobed or irregularly toothed. The strongly lemon-scented flowers are very numerous, $\frac{3}{4}$in (18mm) across, with five to eight narrow and silky, greenish-yellow sepals in large rounded panicles.

C. colensoi and *C. parviflora* are very similar; even *C. australis*, which has white or yellowish flowers, has similar foliage. All are so variable that even botanists have difficulty in distinguishing them at times. They have survived on sheltered walls in the southwest of England; in a conservatory or greenhouse they cause no problems, although I feel there are more rewarding climbers for such sites.

Flowers: June
Height: 8–12ft (2.4–3.6m)
Pruning category: A

C. fusca
Country of origin: Hokkaido to Siberia, 1860

I re-introduced this species from Japan. This is no brightly garbed seductress, its fascination more tactile than visual, but never to be ignored. For some years *C. japonica* was distributed as this species but it is hard to imagine how such a distinctive flower could ever be confused with any other, even though a similar rounded urn-shape is found in a number of the American species, although not so constricted at the mouth. The four sepals are distinctively ribbed, the tips recurving to show the pale green interior; although the sepal colour is purple, this is almost totally obscured by thick, woolly dark brown hairs. The flowers are terminal and axillary, with a pair of small bracts about the flower stalk. The 6–9in (15–23cm) leaves divide into five to nine leaflets, ovate and entire, although some are broadly lobed.

Extremely hardy, this climber forms a woody framework unless pruned hard annually.

Flowers: July
Height: 8–10ft (2.4–3m)
Pruning category: C

C. fusca var. *glabricalyx*

This variety is far less hairy and consequently the sepal colour is visible, appearing as a metallic bronze-purple.

Opposite above: *C. florida* 'Alba Plena'; opposite below: *C. florida* 'Sieboldii'

C. fusca

C. fusca (dwarf form)

In 1981 I received from a friend in Japan plants that had been collected from the mountain area of Hokkaido. Identical in all respects to the type species except that it is quite dwarf, reaching only 1ft 6in to 2ft (45–60cm) in height; it is of non-clinging habit and flowers about a month earlier.

As no previous mention has been made of this variety, it appears to be a formerly unknown subspecies and should prove an interesting addition to the range of hardy herbaceous clematis.

C. gentianoides
Country of origin: Tasmania

A most charming little plant with prostrate evergreen stems 1ft to 1ft 6in (30–45cm) long. The leathery leaves are simple, lanceolate and up to 2in (5cm) long, smooth or with a few small teeth; they are dark green in colour, tinged bronze; the young foliage is quite purple.

The pure white cruciform flowers, with yellow anthers, are 2in (5cm) across and are borne singly from the terminal axils. The trailing stems turn upwards at the tips just before flowering, which gives the impres-sion of myriads of white stars sitting just above the ground. A most unclematis-looking plant, which con-fuses the majority of visitors.

It is difficult to say just how hardy it is. It has sur-vived normal winters, but has yet to be tested in a hard one; it would be prudent to give it winter protection.

Flowers: July–September
Pruning category: A

C. heracleifolia
Country of origin: China, 1837

A stiff semi-herbaceous perennial having stout stems and very large leaves; it does not die completely back to the ground but forms a woody base. The leaves are a noticeable feature; they are divided into three, the cen-tral lobe being wide and ovate, and twice the size, up to 6in (15cm) long and 4in (10cm) wide, shallowly toothed and slightly hairy.

The flowers are remarkably like those of a hyacinth; they are borne on short stalks, in circular fashion, from the axils on the upper parts of the stems. The four sepals are formed into a 1in (2.5cm) tube, recurved at the tips, light to purplish-blue in colour. The plant is mono-ecious, bearing separate male and female flowers.

All the wild forms that I have seen have been inferior to the better known, and more desirable, named varieties.

Flowers: August–September
Height: 3ft (90cm)
Pruning category: C

C. heracleifolia 'Campanile'
Hybridizer: unknown

This plant was originally purchased under the guise of 'Côte d'Azur', but subsequent investigation revealed that Côte d'Azur' is a totally different plant and probably lost to cultivation.

It accords most closely with an old illustration and description of 'Campanile', the only origin of which is given as 'of French gardens', and it is most probably a selected form of *C. heracleifolia*, differing but little from the type species. The flowers are slightly larger, and the lavender-blue tube is deeper at the tips, paling inside. A slight scent is detectable; the plant is also taller growing.

Flowers: August–September
Height: 4ft (1.5m)
Pruning category: C

C. heracleifolia 'Wyevale'

C. heracleifolia 'Davidiana'
Country of origin: China, 1864

Those gardeners whose sense of smell is below par, should have no problems here – the scent is heavy, almost overpoweringly so, and more agreeable from a distance.

The flowers are a clear lavender-blue throughout, longer and opening wider at the mouth than in the type species. They are more numerous, too, and borne in dense rounded clusters from the upper axils. They are dioecious (male and female flowers on different plants), although I have only come across the male form. The plant does not form woody basal shoots, but grows into a soft expanding clump from underground shoots.

Flowers: August–September
Height: 3ft (90cm)
Pruning category: C

C. heracleifolia 'Wyevale'
Hybridizer: unknown

This superb variety makes a most distinguished-looking border plant. The mid-blue sepals reflex from midway down the tube and roll back on themselves.

Not only are the flowers larger than those of *C. Davidiana,* but the ends of the sepals are wider, with pretty frilled edges. They are borne from near ground level round every node up to the uppermost terminal cluster. This, like *C. heracleifolia* 'Davidiana', is a male form with prominent yellow stamens.

It is rather unfortunate that a form marketed under this name has small flowers similar to *C. heracleifolia* itself, except that they are deep blue.

Flowers: August–September
Height: 3ft (90cm)
Pruning category: C

C. hexasepala
Country of origin: New Zealand, 1818

An evergreen climber, *C. hexasepala* is, in common with other New Zealand clematis, dioecious. The white flowers resemble smaller versions of *C. indivisa,* being 1–1½in (2.5–4cm) in diameter. The leaves are 3–5in (8–13cm) long, triternate, each leaflet so deeply and irregularly lobed as to appear almost partially eaten or nibbled; the terminal lobe is long and finger-like. The foliage goes through the same changing phases, from juvenile to adult, as *C. indivisa.* A smaller, more slender climber and more suited to a small conservatory.

Flowers: March–April
Height: 6–8ft (1.8–2.4m)
Pruning category: A

C. × huldine
Hybridizer: Morel, c.1900

C. × huldine could be, and often is, listed with the large-flowered hybrids, but I prefer to keep it separate as it is such a distinctive plant. The 4in (10cm) flower is composed of six sepals incurved along their length, the tips turned over in a most charming way, not overlapping. The upper surface, which faces skywards, is white with an unusual pearly lustre; on the underside is a purple-mauve wash, deeper along the midrib, which, as the flower is translucent, appears as a pale pink bar on the upper surface. The small stamens are greenish-cream. The leaves are divided into five leaflets.

A most vigorous clematis, it flowers with equal vigour. It can, however, fail to flower at all in some gardens, and it would be wise to plant in a warm, sunny position. This endearing plant looks best planted where it can be viewed from below, and it will clamber into a small tree, or over a large pergola or wall. It would have been interesting to have known the parentage. There is probably some texensis blood and I would also guess viticella,

but what of the others? And which contributed to its upward-facing flowers?

Flowers: July–September
Height: 10–15ft (3–4.5m)
Pruning category: C

C. indivisa
Country of origin: New Zealand, 1840

It is almost inevitable that a plant with the near-perfect combination of neat, evergreen foliage, compact habit and utter freedom of flowering should have some disadvantage. It has, unless a corner of a sheltered wall can be provided, and then only in the milder areas. Grown in a cold conservatory, however, this problem can be overcome and a spectacular show guaranteed. A straightforward, simple beauty that can stand on its own merit and is best left to do so.

In common with most of the New Zealand clematis, the foliage goes through a fairly long process of changing leaf shape, from the long, narrow, lance-shape of the juvenile years to the adult trifoliate, ovate and blunt-ended leaflets. They are leathery but less glossy than those of *C. armandii.*

C. indivisa var. *lobata* is sometimes offered for sale; this is merely *C. indivisa* at the second- and third-year leaf stage, with attractive lobed leaves, but, as it is not a fixed clone, it will eventually change to adult foliage.

Male and female flowers are borne on different plants, in large axillary panicles so abundant as almost to hide the foliage. The male flower is comprised of six to eight glistening white sepals, 3in (8cm) across and blunt-ended; the anthers are orange-pink. The more abundant female flowers are smaller, 2in (5cm) across, with sterile green filaments.

Flowers: May–June
Height: 10–15ft (3–4.5m)
Pruning category: A

C. integrifolia
Country of origin: southern Europe, 1573

This is one of the few herbaceous clematis that most gardeners can confidently name. From a gradually expanding clump, a mass of thin stems rise annually, each terminating in a solitary nodding flower. This is composed of four sepals, each narrowly ovate, 1in (2.5cm) long and tapering to sharp points, forming a loose, disarranged bell. It is thick and fleshy in texture, but much less so than the American viornae. The colour can vary

Opposite: *C. indivisa* (female flowers)

in intensity but is commonly purple-blue, deeper and richer near the stalk. The stamens are creamy-white and tightly packed, and the stalkless leaves 3–6in (8–15cm) long, are lanceolate-ovate.

Under certain conditions the plants stand erect of their own accord. However, the stems usually fall against whatever happens to be nearby; in an open border they collapse on to the ground, with the terminal 1ft (30cm) turning upwards again. The following named varieties all have more rewarding qualities than the species.

Flowers: July
Height: 3ft (90cm)
Pruning category: C

C. integrifolia 'Alba'

White forms have always occasionally occurred among wild stands. Always uncommon, it is now quite rare in cultivation. The flowers are borne terminally and, although white, shade to pale blue near the stalks.

Flowers: July
Height: 3ft (90cm)
Pruning category: C

C. integrifolia 'Hendersonii'

Virtually from the time of its introduction, integrifolia was recorded as having various colour forms, although most of the original ones have disappeared.

This is an old selection, identical to the type plant in colour and form, but the flower is almost twice as large.

Flowers: July
Height: 3ft (90cm)
Pruning category: C

C. integrifolia 'Olgae'

The superiority of the named varieties is more than a matter of colour; they have the advantage of multiple flower heads as opposed to the solitary one in the wild species.

This variety has comparatively large flowers, 1½in (4cm) deep and 2in (5cm) across; the sepals curve out and upwards in the manner of a martagon (Turk's cap) lily, and 10–12 flowers are borne on each stem. The mid-blue colour is attractive and the scent delicious.

Flowers: July–August
Height: 2ft (60cm)
Pruning category: C

C. integrifolia 'Pastel Blue'

This and its companion, 'Pastel Pink', were released in the same year, 1986. The flowers are large and of the same martagon-lily shape as 'Olgae' and are sweetly scented. They are a clear, light blue and are borne in groups of 10–12 to a head.

Flowers: July–August
Height: 2ft (60cm)
Pruning category: C

C. integrifolia 'Pastel Pink'

The scented, light pink flowers, shaped like loosely-formed bells, are borne in clusters.

Flowers: July–August
Height: 2ft (60cm)
Pruning category: C

C. integrifolia 'Rosea'

Both white and pink varieties have been mentioned from the earliest days, and in 'Rosea' we have not just a fine integrifolia, but one of the most beautiful of herbaceous plants and undoubtedly one of my favourites.

The pink colouring is bright and clear, the long, slightly twisted sepals delightfully crimped along the edges to form a most captivating shape. As with other integrifolias, the sepals are heavily ribbed, particularly around the base where the deep pink colour is also more concentrated. Internally, the pink is much paler but still most conspicuous as the flower grows to about 2in (5cm) across; the stamens are deep yellow. The flowers are borne singly, not in clusters like some integrifolias, but later flowers are produced from the axillary buds.

Flowers: July–August
Height: 2ft (60cm)
Pruning category: C

C. integrifolia 'Tapestry'

The most recent release, and, although not cluster forming, it does have axillary buds. I thought the colour justifiable enough to overcome this. A red integrifolia will come some time in the future; until then, this is the nearest to that colour. The flower is large and spreading, a strange mauve-red deepening towards the stalk into a bright brocade-red; on the inside, the sepals are a paler dusky mauve-pink.

Flowers: July–August
Height: 2–3ft (60–90cm)
Pruning category: C

C. integrifolia 'Hendersonii'

C. japonica

Country of origin: Japan

This charming, though rarely seen, species has the nodding urn-shape typical of the viornae type, although the 1in (2.5cm) long flowers soon open out into campanulate bells. They are purplish-red or brownish-red and so polished as to look like burnished mahogany. The tips of the four fleshy sepals recurve to expose the pale green inside, which is finely spotted with brown-red; along the edges is a fine white, woolly line.

The flowers are borne in short-stemmed clusters of one to five, from the axils of the previous year's growth, each having two little bracts halfway along the stalk. On close inspection the flowers are most striking, but unfortunately they tend to be obscured by the foliage. The leaves are ternate, with 2–3in (5–8cm) long, coarsely serrated leaflets.

Flowers: May–June
Height: 6–10ft (1.8–3m)
Pruning category: B

C. japonica 'Gokonosho'

One of the joys of gardening is the gift of plants from others, often unexpected, occasionally tremendously exciting. Such a plant was 'Gokonosho', which was found by a friend in Japan as a small seedling growing on a mountainside and despatched to me in the hope that I could propagate from it.

Unlike some other genera, which seem to have no inhibitions about producing variegated foliage in various shadings of white, cream or yellow, clematis are particularly shy in this respect. 'Gokonosho' was the first truly variegated clematis I had seen in over 25 years of growing and studying these plants. The leaves are marvellously splashed and mottled with creamy-white and pale green, some divided down the centre into two distinct colours. The flowers are the usual brownish-red and create a far better contrast than they do against the normal green.

Drawbacks have become apparent unfortunately; the shoots often revert to green, and the plant itself is far less easy to grow than the type.

Flowers: May–June
Height: 6ft (1.8m)
Pruning category: B

Opposite: *C. integrifolia* 'Rosea'

C. × jouiniana and *C. × jouiniana* 'Praecox'

Hybridizer: unknown

It is a sad fact that many garden-worthy plants never achieve the popularity they deserve simply because they need to be seen in a garden environment. Some can achieve almost overnight success purely by being photogenic or suited to a garden-centre impulse buy.

A hardy and easy plant, × *jouiniana* offers little more enticement from a photograph than from a catalogue description and must be seen to be appreciated. The only hybrid from our native *C. vitalba*, the other parent assumed to be *C. heracleifolia* var. 'Davidiana', it was raised in France around 1900. Individually, the flowers are not exciting, 1½–2in (4–5cm) across, with four, five or six narrow sepals reflexed at the tips; they are off-white in colour, with mauve-blue tips to the sepals, and the outside, too, is in this deeper colour. They are borne in terminal and axillary panicles of about 20 flowers along the upper 2–4ft (0.6–1.2m) of growth and give an overall impression of a huge, misty blue, leafy panicle.

As could be expected from the parentage, the leaves are large, divided into three to five 4in (10cm) leaflets, coarsely toothed. This hardly matters for the flowers are so numerous as to almost obscure them. Incidentally, very few clematis are considered for their autumn-coloured foliage, but *C. × jouiniana* turns a golden-yellow instead of the usual 'green going-on dead' look.

This is a non-clinging sub-shrub, forming a woody framework from the first few feet of growth; it is better pruned back to this woody growth rather than to ground level. I grow it down a bank where it looks marvellous, but it will look equally good over a shrub, tree stump or fence. *C. × jouiniana* itself is rarely grown now as the variey 'Praecox' starts earlier and gives an extra four to six weeks of flower.

Flowers: July–October
Height: 6–10ft (1.8–3 m)
Pruning category: C

C. ladakhiana

Country of origin: Kashmir

In 1980 I received from Kew Gardens a plant with this name, which appears to be a newly collected species. L.H.J. Williams (formerly Department of Botany, British Museum) who has done so much work with plants from the Himalayas has been unable to find any reference to the name. It does, however, have a close affinity to the thibetana and orientalis group.

The leaves, 4–6in (10–15cm) long, are divided into five to seven, ¼in (6mm) wide, narrow, lanceolate leaflets, some with both or only one side deeply incised;

C. japonica 'Gokonosho'

they are glaucous, but less so than those of thibetana. The four sepals are 1in (2.5cm) long and $\frac{3}{8}$in (9mm) wide, tapering to fine, slightly upturned points. They form a nodding open bell, of the most unusual old-gold colour, finely peppered inside and out with dark red speckles. The stamens are conspicuous, with deep maroon filaments and dull yellow anthers.

Intriguing rather than showy, it is a very popular plant with flower arrangers. It has proved to be hardy, but it does require plenty of sun to flower well and consequently may be too late for more northerly areas.

Flowers: August–October
Height: 15ft (4.5m)
Pruning category: C

C. macropetala
Country of origin: China, 1829

Ask any nurseryman who specializes in one particular type of plant what is the question most often put to him and it is undoubtedly: 'If you had to choose one, which is your favourite?' That is, of course, an impossible question to answer; a favourite one year may not necessarily be so the next; even last month's star soon

recedes as another takes the stage. If I had to choose but one clematis, it would be C. macropetala, although I would still have to cheat a little and add its colour variations.

You may well think that there is a long wait between each short flowering season. True, but such a gem is worth such a wait. I may be prejudiced because this was one of the first clematis I grew and, on practical grounds, one that comes through the severest winters unscathed, never failing to put on one of the first displays of spring.

This species, the alpinas and other relatives are sometimes classed as a separate group, the atragenes. They are all distinguished by having a number of staminodes between the stamens and the sepals. In macropetala, the outer rows are elongated to form a spiky, double, nodding open bell, $2\frac{1}{2}$–3in (6–8cm) across; these outer staminodes can vary from six, in a poor form, to as many as 20, and they are a similar colour to the sepals; the inner, shorter staminodes are off-white to pure white. In nature, the colour is pale blue with purple-blue shading. As most of the plants on offer are grown from seed, the colour is almost as variable as the shape, and although

Opposite above: C. × jouiniana 'Praecox'; opposite below: C. ladakhiana

there may be no poor macropetalas, there are certainly good ones; it is advisable to see the plants in flower.

The foliage is neat and attractive, the biternate leaves sharply serrated and unfolding simultaneously with the flowers. As with all the atragenes, macropetala seems to delight in a cooler, shadier aspect. Do not be put off, however, if your garden is wholly sunny, because it will do equally well. The seed-heads are a feature, lasting well into the winter.

Although discovered and grown in Europe for many years previously, *C. macropetala* did not reach Britain until 1910.

Flowers: April–May
Height: 6–8ft (1.8–2.4m)
Pruning category: A

C. macropetala 'Louise'
Hybridizer: Fretwell, 1983

This form of *C. macropetala* has delicate, pale rose sepals and staminodes and a deep cyclamen-pink stain near the stem.

C. macropetala 'Madeleine'
Hybridizer: Fretwell, 1982

The sepals are deep purple, a little less deep on the outer staminodes.

C. macropetala 'Markham's Pink'
Hybridizer: Markham, 1935

A good, full and spiky flower, looking pinker in the mass than in the individual flower. The outside of the four sepals are a deep rose-mauve pink, while the undersides and long staminodes are a softer, dusky pink.

C. macropetala 'Snowbird'
Hybridizer: Fretwell, 1969

This clematis unfailingly captivates me afresh each year with its elegant purity; after 20 years it is still the clematis for which I hold most affection. I may be biased, but others must have been equally enchanted for it is now widely established in numerous countries. Unfortunately, its popularity has led to its being sold under different names, mainly abroad.

The flowers are maybe more open than in macropetala

C. macropetala

itself; the sepals and the first 15 or so long spiky staminodes are pure white, the inner cluster of smaller ones greenish-white. The foliage is pale green, while the stems and young growth are yellow-green. It is vigorous enough, but slower to become established and not as tall as the other macropetalas. In common with them, however, a small flush of flower is quite common in the autumn.

Flowers: May
Height: 6ft (1.8m)
Pruning category: A

C. montana

Country of origin: Himalayas, 1831

The ubiquitous montana, so often the first clematis to be purchased, or just as likely, given as it is the easiest of the genus to grow and to propagate. It is so vigorous that, planted in the wrong position, it can be an embarrassment; in the right one, it is capable of masking or softening the most obtrusive outlines.

The flowers are white. There is no such plant as montana 'Alba', which is how most of the Dutch imports seem to be labelled; the same applies to 'Odorata', which was merely one of the early names for montana. Most forms are strongly vanilla-scented, but it would be wise to enquire before buying. The same goes for flower size and colour. They are normally 2–2½in (5–6cm), the four sepals may be narrow or wide, white or grubby white, with pale cream stamens, and borne in axillary clusters. While it is usual for it to smother itself in blossom, some forms are not so forthcoming. The leaves, which are ternate, are sharply pointed and ovate with coarse serrations.

Unless otherwise stated, the following named varieties reach the same height, and flower at the same time and should be pruned at the same time and in the same way as montana itself.

Flowers: May–June
Height: 20–30ft (6–9m)
Pruning category: A

C. montana 'Alexander'

This is a most attractive flower if you are prepared for a long wait to see it. As it takes five or six years to settle into flowering, we now only propagate to order. The flowers are 3in (8cm) across, well-shaped, creamy-white and strongly scented. It is a vigorous grower.

C. macropetala 'Snowbird'

C. montana 'Continuity'

Hybridizer: unknown

I have placed this variety under montana due to lack of evidence as regards its breeding, although the foliage bears characteristics attributable to C. chrysocoma (see page 97). The leaves are large, coarsely serrated, similar to a green version of 'Tetrarose' (see page 124), but with a slightly softer outline. Both these and the young shoots have a covering of fine hairs.

Although the flowers come in spring, along with other montanas, this remarkable variety does not finish there. After a lapse of approximately six weeks the quickly extending new growth will continuously produce more flowers in twos and threes, on 10–12in (25–30cm) stalks until stopped by autumn frosts. They are a pleasant shade of rose-pink and have conspicuously large, creamy-white stamens. It is, however, not as vigorous as a normal montana.

Flowers: May, and July–October
Height: 15–20ft (4.5–6m)
Pruning category: A

C. montana 'Elizabeth'

A well-shaped flower. The four wide and slightly cupped sepals are a rather pale, clear pink, and the flowers have a vanilla scent. Young foliage is tinged with purple. Another vigorous grower.

C. montana 'Grandiflora'

Pure white, with wide sepals and flowers 3in (8cm) across. There are different forms of this variety, some of which are scented. I have seen C. spooneri sold under this label.

C. montana 'Peveril'

Country of origin: China, 1979

In old literature on clematis, C. montana 'Wilsonii' keeps appearing as the autumn-flowering montana. With so many similar descriptions there must have been such a plant, though it would seem long lost to cultivation. A few years ago, we were sent seed of a montana that must be close to the old 'Wilsonii'. I believe that this could be one of the most exciting finds to enter the horticultural world for many years. The flowering period in the south-west of England extends from about the middle to the end of July; farther north it would probably run into August. The flowers are large for a montana, 3in (8cm) across, the four sepals obovate, wide across the blunt tips but gappy. The colour is pure white, and one of its most striking features is one not found in the old 'Wilsonii', namely a boss of the longest stamens I have seen in any clematis. The long, thread-like filaments, with yellow stamens, shimmer as strongly as in any hypericum or eucryphia. Unfortunately it does not possess any scent, while 'Wilsonii' was described as strongly scented. The flowers are borne on the old wood, as in other montanas; by the time the display begins, the plant is a mass of new growth, although the blooms are not obscured by the foliage as they are borne on 12–15in (30–38cm) long flower stalks.

As befits a montana so different from the rest of its kin, the foliage, too, is markedly distinctive. Although the ternate leaves are serrated, they are more blunt, giving a soft, rounded outline. The area between the veins is raised, creating a textured, quilted effect, with sparse silver hair. Although the plant is sturdy enough it is far less vigorous than the type plant.

Flowers: July
Height: 15–20ft (4.5–6m)
Pruning category: A

C. montana 'Picton's Variety'

An exceptional variety. The flowers are very full, some having five or six sepals, coloured deep rose-mauve with cream stamens, and with a pleasant spicy scent. Its less vigorous growth makes it suitable for small gardens and areas usually precluded from hosting the normal montanas. The leaves are a handsome bronze-green colour.

Height: 15–20ft (4.5–6m)

C. montana 'Rubens'

Country of origin: China, 1900

This is even more variable in colour than the type plant, sometimes so pale as to appear dirty-white when seen

Opposite above: C. montana 'Peveril'; opposite below: C. montana 'Picton's Variety'

en masse. In its better forms it should be a deep lavender-pink or mauve-pink, with creamy stamens. There is a vanilla-scent. The leaves, especially on the new growth, are purple-tinged.

An exceptionally severe winter can kill montanas, older plants appearing to be more susceptible than young ones, but this particular variety is somewhat hardier; two plants in England's Peak District, with stems 5in (12cm) thick, were planted in the early 1900s and still look remarkably healthy.

C. montana 'Tetrarose'

This tetraploid variety originated in Holland and has been widely distributed from there. The flowers are larger than usual, 3in (8cm) across, the four sepals wide and bowl-shaped. It is an attractive rose-pink and has creamy stamens; the scent, a spicy cedarwood, is similar to 'Picton's Variety'. The bronze-green leaves too, are large, ternate, each leaflet sharply pointed and heavily serrated. It is not as prolific as some.

Height: 20ft (6m)

C. montana 'Wilsonii'
Country of origin: China, 1900

This starts its display four to five weeks later than others of the species. When fully developed, the creamy-white flowers are 2½in (6cm) across, although the sepals are narrow. Wait for the flowers to expand as, initially, they are small, grubby little things. Apart from its later flowering, it has a most distinctive chocolate scent.

Flowers: June–July
Height: 30ft (9m)

C. nepalensis
Country of origin: Nepal, China, 1912

Another species that was discovered and grown years before it was introduced into Britain. Although it is usually described as evergreen, this is something of a misnomer, winter green being a more accurate description. It has the strange habit of losing its leaves at the onset of summer, when it has the appearance of a dead plant until new growth starts again about October.

The leaves look delicate, not of the leathery texture usually expected on winter-borne foliage; ternate with 1–3in (2.5–8cm) lanceolate leaflets, once or twice lobed, they are bright green and abundantly produced. The flowers are pale coloured but attract attention in mid-winter when there is little or no competition. Borne in short-stemmed clusters from the axils, the ½in (12mm) long bells are similar in shape and size to the better known *C. rehderiana* (see page 128). They are creamy-white and silky-textured, with a small, cup-shaped bract above the base of the flower; the rich purple stamens are outstanding, protruding well beyond the bell.

Not reliably hardy, it requires a sheltered wall, and that in the warmer parts of the country only.

Flowers: January–March
Height: 25ft (7.5m)
Pruning category: A

C. ochotensis
Country of origin: Japan, c.1880

This is the Japanese equivalent of the European *C. alpina*, having similar biternate, coarsely-toothed leaflets. The flowers, too, are very close to alpina, except for the blunt tips to the sepals; they are pinkish-lilac to rosy-purple, with creamy-white staminodes. It is extremely hardy and flowers later than *C. alpina*.

Flowers: May–June
Height: 6ft (1.8m)
Pruning category: A

C. ochreleuca
Country of origin: USA, 1767

A herbaceous perennial, forming a clump of slender stems, each terminating in a solitary, nodding flower, with axillary buds flowering later. Each flower is a 1½in (4cm) elongated bell shape, narrowing to the mouth where the four, rather fleshy sepals widen and the tips roll back. On opening, the colour is bright yellow-green, particularly on the inside, gradually fading to creamy-yellow; the outside is downy with a light purple stain near the stem. The leaves are simple, widely ovate, smooth or with occasional small teeth. An easy-going plant with no particular foibles and a quiet, unassuming charm.

Flowers: June–July
Height: 1ft 6in–2ft (45–60cm)
Pruning category: C

C. orientalis 'Bill Mackenzie'
Hybridizer: unknown

I would rank this as one of the finest clematis ever raised, and certainly the brightest and most showy of the yellow-flowered varieties. Bill Mackenzie, one-time curator at London's Chelsea Physic Garden, said that although the seed came from *C. orientalis* 'L & S 13342'

(see below), he could not guarantee the pollen parent but believed it possibly to be *C. tangutica* (see page 131). That is probably correct, as that cross was used to produce a virtually identical hybrid.

For an orientalis the flowers are large – 3in (8cm) across the mouth of the open nodding bells. The four fleshy sepals, ¾in (18mm) wide and tapering to fine, slightly upturned points, are borne singly or three to a 6–8in (15–20cm) stalk from almost every axil so that the entire plant is a mass of yellow. The sepals have a shiny, waxy appearance and are roughly textured like orange peel. The foliage, though, is less attractive, having inherited the bright green colour and, unfortunately, the coarseness attributable to tangutica. The leaves are up to 9in (23cm) long, divided into seven or nine leaflets, again divided into three and serrated.

C. tangutica has always been the clematis grown for its large, silvery seed-heads, but those of 'Bill Mackenzie' are equally fine and, because of the long flowering season, silver and gold are mixed in varying proportions as the season progresses. The seed-heads last well into the new year before winter gales finally tear them loose. Grown over an established hedge or a fence where it can ramble at will then, it will, with light pruning, begin to flower in midsummer and continue unabated until autumn. If hard pruned to keep it to 10–12ft (3–3.6m), flowering will be about a month later.

C. nepalensis

An unfortunate recent aspect is the large number of pseudo seed-raised 'Bill Mackenzie's being offered. Check before you buy.

Flowers: June–October
Height: 10–25ft (3–7.5m)
Pruning category: C

C. orientalis 'L & S 13342'
Country of origin: Himalayas, 1947

For all of its admirable qualities, the bold yellow flamboyance of *C. orientalis* 'Bill Mackenzie' (see above) may not be to everyone's taste. An alternative or addition (for it is not merely a question of choosing between one or the other) is *C. orientalis* 'L & S 13342'. Ludlow and Sherrif collected this fine variety during their 1947 expedition, and it is unusual for the collectors' number to remain. This is a much softer yellow, gradually changing to ochre-yellow. The nodding, spherical flower buds look like berries until the four sepals separate to reveal one of the outstanding characteristics of this plant, their ⅛in (3mm) thick fleshy texture. It is this feature that has led some nurseries to attach names such as 'Orange peel' or 'Lemon peel' clematis. Plants named as 'Orange peel' are

C. orientalis 'Bill Mackenzie'

no guarantee of the true variety because, as with 'Bill Mackenzie', many of them are grown from seed, thereby losing a lot of the original characteristics.

The foliage is infinitely superior to that of 'Bill Mackenzie', the five to nine leaflets on each sub-divided leaf presenting a grey-green, lace-like effect. The seed-heads, however, though showy are not as spectacular. It is vigorous, but I have lost plants after a drought, and watering must be watched; it needs full sun to flower well.

Flowers: July–September
Height: 10–20ft (3–6m)
Pruning category: C

C. × 'Pagoda'

Hybridizer: Treasures, 1980

No doubt in consideration of the commercial value in a popular name, the raisers decided to call this variety *C. texensis* × 'Pagoda'. The parentage is a seedling from *C. texensis* 'Etoile Rose' pollinated by *C. viticella*. As texensis 'Etoile Rose' is, itself, only one-fourth part texensis, some of the large-flowered hybrids have more texensis blood than this.

Its mainly viticella blood shows in the identical growth habit and foliage. The flowers are an intriguing shape, nodding 3in (8cm) bells, the final half of each of the four sepals sweeping upwards in the manner of *C. integrifolia* 'Olgae'. The off-white ground-colour has a reddish-mauve broad band on the outside, and on the inside the veins are picked out in the same reddish-mauve.

Flowers: July–September
Height: 10ft (3m)
Pruning category: C

C. phlebantha

Country of origin: Nepal, 1952

Among the very few clematis which could qualify as purely foliage plants, this species, discovered on the Polunin, Sykes and Williams expedition to Nepal, must rank among the finest.

The 3in (8cm) leaves are neat, divided into five to nine leaflets, the terminal one larger, and all finely dissected, they are grey-green but appear paler as the upper surfaces are covered in silvery fine hairs. It is the undersides, however, that show this characteristic more fully: they are so densely covered in fine down that they appear like little silvery-white mirrors glistening in the sun. Although non-clinging, the thick

stems can fling themselves over surrounding shrubs to a distance of 6ft (1.8m) or so. On a warm wall, assuming that the top growth survives the winters, it will probably double this distance. It does need to keep its top growth to have any chance of bearing flowers, as these are borne on side-shoots off the previous year's growth. Even then, they are not freely produced, each 1–1½in (1–4cm) flower consisting of six white sepals with pronounced pinkish veins.

I am not sure how far north it will prove to be hardy, although L.H.J. Williams, who discovered it and grows it on the edge of England's Dartmoor, manages to keep its top growth through the winter. It definitely needs a well-drained soil and as warm a spot as can be provided.

Flowers: June–August
Height: 4–10ft (1.2–3m)
Pruning category: B

C. pitcheri

Country of origin: USA, 1878

The pitcher-shaped flowers of this species resemble those of C. crispa (see page 100), but they are smaller and narrower, and the tips less rolled back. One of the most noticeable features is the pronounced, heavily ribbed sepals, lavender or rosy-lavender on the outside; usually

C. phlebantha

the inside colour is deep matt purple, although I have a form with a deep ruby interior. The rich cream stamens contrast well.

The 4–6in (10–15cm) leaves are each divided into seven or nine leaflets, the first pair three-lobed, others occasionally lobed as opposed to the smoothness of C. crispa. It is also a more vigorous grower, best planted near a path or border as it is one for close appreciation rather than making an impact from a distance.

Flowers: July–September
Height: 6–10ft (1.8–3m)
Pruning category: C

C. recta

Country of origin: Europe, 1597

Most species that have been in cultivation for a long time vary considerably in quality. This herbaceous perennial varies in height from 3ft to 6ft (90–180cm), usually closer to the latter. Unless it is tied to some support, it will flop over and on to its neighbours. Individually, the white flowers are ¾–1½in (18–30mm) across, cruciform; they are borne in large terminal and axillary panicles during June and July. The number of flowers can differ considerably between good and poor forms. Stems and foliage are smooth and a rich dark green; the leaves are pinnate, 6in (15cm) long, each of the five to seven leaflets ovate. Strangely, although this can be among the most scented of flowers, some forms have not a vestige of scent.

Flowers: June–July
Height: 3–6ft (90–180cm)
Pruning category: C

C. recta 'Peveril'

A selected 'dwarf' form, with thick and strong stems. The flowers are not only large, some having five or six sepals, but they are borne from virtually every axil, so that the entire plant is one frothy white mound and delightfully scented.

Flowers: June–July
Height: 3ft (1m)
Pruning category: C

C. recta 'Purpurea'

This extends the season of interest with young shoots and leaves of a deep bronze-purple, ageing to bronze-green. At present, this clematis is available only in a taller form.

Flowers: June–July
Height: Up to 6ft (1.8m)
Pruning category: C

C. rehderiana

Country of origin: western China

It may seem an anomaly that a plant having large foliage and small flowers could ever be described as showy, but this is.

It is nearly always recommended for growing into a small tree, a job it will do admirably, but many gardeners are deterred by the thought of some kind of large-leaved montana taking over the garden. Some of the most attractive specimens I have seen have been on walls. Cut hard back to around 2ft (60cm) each spring, it will cover an area of some 8–10ft (2.4–3m) in height and as much in spread. The joy of this growing method is that the flowers all face towards you and at just the right height to savour that delicious fragrance; it is a sweet, slightly tangy scent, reminiscent to some of cowslips, to me of mock orange (philadelphus).

The same treatment will enable it to do nicely on a large shrub. If you want to cover a small tree, 15–20ft (4.5–6m) high, do not prune annually or it will never make it. For some reason, young plants are slow to get started and may initially make small bushy thickets; eventually they will get going.

A deciduous climber, growing strongly to 20ft (6m) if unpruned when it tends to bunch together rather than spread over the canopy of a tree like a montana. Stems are angled, almost square in section. The pinnate leaves, with five, seven or nine leaflets, are ovate, cordate, moderately toothed and slightly lobed at the base, 2–3in (5–8cm) long and 2in (5cm) wide; they are downy on the upper surfaces, with pronounced veins on the undersides; the stalks and stems are covered in stiff hairs.

Flowers are borne in panicles up to 10in (25cm) in length, pointing up and outwards at an angle of 60 degrees irrespective of how the stems are growing. Individually, they are small, nodding bells, about $\frac{1}{2}$in (12mm) long, true primrose-yellow on opening but quickly fading to pale parchment. They have four sepals, the tips recurving to touch the outside of the bell, which is velvety in texture with small raised ribs on the outside, but smooth within.

Flowers: July–September
Height: 20ft (6m)
Pruning category: C

C. serratifolia

Country of origin: Manchuria, Japan, Korea, 1918

Although it has a rather short flowering season, this remains one of my favourite species. Usually described as looking like a tangutica, it bears little, if any, resemblance to it. The four pointed sepals are wide, opening obliquely into an open nodding bell, $1\frac{1}{2}$–2in (4–5cm) across the mouth, and looking remarkably like C. alpina in form. They are ribbed on the outside and textured on the inner surface. The colour is a clear primrose-yellow with contrasting purple stamens; the flowers are borne singly or three to a stalk from the axils. Often described as strongly scented, there must be forms more scented than mine as the lemon scent is only faintly perceptible.

The light green leaves are biternate, each leaflet coarsely serrated, 2–3in (5–8cm) long. It is nothing like as rampant a grower as C. orientalis, but the seed heads are equally attractive.

Flowers: August–September
Height: 8–12ft (2.4–3.6m)
Pruning category: C

Opposite above: C. pitcheri; opposite below C. recta 'Peveril'

C. speciosa
Country of origin: Japan

I sometimes wonder if this species, which has often been confused with *C. stans* (see below), has in the past been responsible for the conflicting descriptions ascribed to that species. Although the stems are thick, they are taller and tend to flop over. The flowers are longer, $\frac{3}{4}$–1in (2–2.5cm), fewer to the panicle and fewer panicles to the stem; the colour is a pale, warm lavender shaded off-white. This species has even larger leaves than *C. stans*, ternate, with leaflets 4–6in (10–15cm) long and 2–4in (5–10cm) wide, the central one two- to three-lobed, with short, rounded teeth.

Flowers: September–October
Height: 3–4ft (1–1.2m)
Pruning category: C

C. spooneri
Country of origin: China, 1909

This has so close an affinity with montana that it could, for garden purposes, be described as a superior form of that species. Equally vigorous and flowering at the same time, the flowers are far superior to any of the other white-flowered montanas. They are fully 3in (8cm) across and produced in clusters from the axils of the previous year's growth; the four round, obovate sepals, with crimped tips, overlap, or nearly so; the stamens are yellow. As so often happens, some loss must be expected at the expense of flower power and, unfortunately, there is not a vestige of scent.

The leaves are ternate, the leaflets broader than in montana, with large, irregular serrations; they are very slightly hairy but nothing like some of the other montana relatives, such as *C. chrysocoma* (see page 97). This leads directly on to one of those tiresome and inexplicable name changes; some taxonomists have proposed that this species have its name changed to *C. chrysocoma* var. *sericea*. I see no reason to change to this as its resemblance to chrysocoma is no nearer than to montana.

Flowers: May–June
Height: 20–30ft (6–9m)
Pruning category: A

C. stans
Country of origin: Japan, 1860

This close relative of *C. heracleifolia* has had rather poor

Opposite above: *C. rehderiana; opposite below: C. serratifolia*

reviews in past literature on clematis. Admittedly, it is not in the top rank, but to deem it of no garden value disregards the good points that it does have.

The flowers are small, narrow tubes, $\frac{3}{4}$in (2cm) long, pale blue and with a covering of short white down; the sepals roll back at the tips to reveal the exquisite sky-blue interior. Borne in long-stalked, loose panicles from most axils on the stiff upright stems, the flowers have a most delicious lily-of-the-valley scent. The large leaves are rather out of proportion to the flowers; they are ternate, with leaflets 2–4in (5–10cm) long and almost as wide, two or three cleft and coarsely toothed.

Flowers: September–October
Height: 2–3ft (60–90cm)
Pruning category: C

C. tangutica
Country of origin: China, 1898

The most commonly grown of the yellow-flowered species, this is, therefore, the most recognizable. At its best, a rich buttercup yellow although, as virtually all plants of tangutica are grown from seed, the depth of colour will vary as will the size of flower to some extent. The flowers are campanulate, 1–1$\frac{1}{2}$in (2.5–4cm) long and nodding; they are borne on 6–8in (15–20cm) stalks, singly or three to a stem from the axils. The seed-heads are spectacular, shining intensely silvery in the sunlight and lasting well into the winter. The stamens are less showy than those of *C. orientalis*, being more of a grubby brownish-purple; the foliage, too, is inferior, the sea-green leaves being divided into five to seven leaflets, some lobed and all irregularly toothed. The species seems to tolerate more shade than *C. orientalis*, but will perform more satisfactorily in sun.

Flowers: July–October
Height: 10–15ft (3–4.5m)
Pruning category: C

C. tangutica var. obtusiuscula

This has smaller, deeper coloured, blunt-tipped flowers. For garden purposes, it appears to show hardly any difference from some of the ordinary forms around.

C. tangutica 'Drake's Form'

This appears to be either a form of *C. chiisanensis* or, possibly, a hybrid between that and *C. tangutica*. It is a rather difficult plant to grow satisfactorily and has the disconcerting habit of suddenly dying for no apparent reason.

C. terniflora
Country of origin: China, Korea, Japan, 1860

If ever a plant suffered from the unwelcome attentions of the horticultural academics, this must come near the top of the list. You may already have it or have seen it listed under any one of the following names: *C. maximowicziana*, *C. paniculata* or *C. dioscoreifolia* var. *robusta*. The two latest Japanese flora list it as *terniflora*, and I have used this name, which is, at least, pronounceable. The plant itself is, in essence, a larger form of the better-known *C. flammula*. The cruciform flowers are white, 1–1½in (4–5cm) across, and have the same hawthorn scent. The leaves are variable in shape and size but commonly dark green, 6in (15cm) long and divided into five smooth, narrowly ovate leaflets. A vigorous plant, it flowers well only after a summer hot enough to ripen the wood.

Flowers: September–October
Height: 20–30ft (6–9m)
Pruning category: C

C. texensis
Country of origin: USA (Texas), 1868

Always a rare plant in cultivation, uncommon even in the wild, few people have had the privilege of growing this species. It is the only species within the genus to have a true red colour, and it is to this that we owe the near-red and pink colouring present in many of the hybrids. The flowers are pitcher-shaped, 1in (2.5cm) long and approximately ¾in (2cm) wide across the base, tapering to half that near the mouth where the four thick, fleshy sepals open out at the tips; they are pointed and do not roll back. The colour is always red; although this can vary from crimson to scarlet-orange, it is never pink nor purplish, and plants of these colours are invariably hybrids between texensis and one of the closely related species. Interestingly the red colour is carried along the flower stalk, even to the point of being more intense than the flower itself. Some of the earliest references describe texensis as shading to creamy-buff in the interior, and it has forever since been thus described. It can, however, be completely red throughout. The yellow stamens are barely visible.

Such an alluring flower deserves attractive foliage, and the smooth, glaucous leaves provide a perfect foil for the scarlet blooms. They are pinnate, with five to nine leaflets although, on some, the terminal leaflet is replaced by a small tendril. Widely cordate, some are almost round, and they have a fine network of raised veins. The species needs a warm, sunny wall and,

Opposite: *C. spooneri*

although in its native home it keeps some top growth, my experience has always been that it dies down to ground level in the winter.

Flowers: July–October
Height: 5–8ft (1.5–2.4m)
Pruning category: C

C. texensis 'Duchess of Albany'
Hybridizer: Jackman, 1890

It is hardly surprising that the introduction of such an exciting species as texensis should have fired the enthusiasm of the early hybridizers. Although, sadly, some of the original crosses have been lost, we are fortunate that at least a few have survived, both from the Continent of Europe and from Britain.

The only British hybridizer to have achieved any success in crossing texensis with other varieties was George Jackman, who, towards the end of the 19th century, crossed texensis with various large-flowered hybrids, which, apart from 'Star of India', he failed to name. The six hybrids resulting from these crosses were 'Admiration', 'Countess of Onslow', 'Duchess of Albany', 'Duchess of York', 'Grace Darling' and 'Sir Trevor Lawrence'. Unless some old plants are hiding somewhere, the only two surviving varieties are 'Duchess of Albany' and 'Sir Trevor Lawrence' (see page 136). Twenty years ago plants of 'Countess of Onslow' were occasionally offered; they fitted the original description of 'Duchess of York' but this, too, seems to have departed the scene. The flowers of all these hybrids have the same elongated bell shape, very similar to kaufmanniana tulips.

'Duchess of Albany' is an attractive shade, a clear pink, with rose-pink bars and cream stamens; the outside is a less intense pink, with paler margins. The four, five or six sepals have a thick, fleshy texture. The leaves resemble more closely those of the texensis parent, divided into three to five small, heart-shaped leaflets, smooth and grey-green.

Flowers: August–October
Height: 6–8ft (1.8–2.4m)
Pruning category: C

C. texensis 'Etoile Rose'
Hybridizer: Lemoine, 1903

I have purposely left this gem among a group of gems until last because, although it is classed as a texensis hybrid, there are noticeable differences. Those already described are texensis F_1 hybrids: they have upward-facing, trumpet-shaped flowers, which benefit from

Opposite above: *C. texensis;* opposite below: *C. texensis*   *C. texensis* 'Etoile Rose'
'Duchess of Albany'

being seen below eye level as the concentration of colour is strongest inside the bell; and they are ideal subjects for scrambling over low-growing shrubs.

Lemoine gave the parentage of this as *C. × globulosa (C. douglasii × C. texensis)* crossed with an unnamed variety of viticella. From this it will be seen that texensis constitutes only 25 per cent of the make-up of 'Etoile Rose' and that viticella has the greater percentage. Indeed, there is a strong resemblance to viticella in the way it holds its nodding flowers, even more in its short, green-tinged stamens and in the virtually indistinguishable foliage. The four sepals have a fleshy texture, with an intensity of colour that could come only from texensis. The flowers are shorter in the tube than other varieties and open into a wide campanulate bell, with recurved tips, about 3in (8cm) across at the mouth. The deep, cherry-pink colour appears on both surfaces, with a pale pink margin on the inside and silver pink on the outside.

As the flowers are nodding, a taller host is needed in order to appreciate the rich colour and textured surface of the interior. It is a marvellous, vigorous variety covered in flower for three months. Rare and choice, it is one of the most sought-after of all clematis; unfortunately, as so often happens, 'Duchess of Albany' (see page 133) has erroneously been sold under this name.

Flowers: July–September
Height: 10–15ft (3–4.5m)
Pruning category: C

C. texensis 'Gravetye Beauty'
Hybridizer: Morel, *c.*1900

Like Jackman, Morel, too, was busy producing texensis hybrids but for some inexplicable reason only one has managed to survive. Morel never seemed to have named any of his hybrids, and William Robinson, great gardener and owner of Gravetye Manor, bestowed this English name upon it. Initially starting the same shape as others in this group, the flower gradually expands into a spidery, open star shape. Both 'Duchess of Albany' (see above) and 'Sir Trevor Lawrence' (see below) open somewhat in the same manner, but not until near sepal-fall. The flowers maintain the rich, ruby-red colour through to sepal-fall; on first opening it has a lustrous satin sheen, which reflects the light in a most distinctive way. The stamens, too, are red; there is not a great deal of colour on the exterior of the sepals.

It is possible for any of these hybrids to keep some of their top growth throughout the winter. They may then start flowering as early as July, although I have found this to be a very rare occurrence.

Flowers: August–October
Height: 6–8ft (1.8–2.4m)
Pruning category: C

C. texensis 'Ladybird Johnson'
Hybridizer: Fretwell, 1984

This is the only other seedling from the same cross responsible for texensis 'The Princess of Wales'; it produced a flower with the same characteristics, except for the colour, which is dusky-red with the edges of the sepals becoming more purple as the flower ages. A particular feature of the sepals is the textured surface and the contrasting cream stamens. Both seedlings have foliage similar to that of other texensis hybrids, but with more tendency to retain some old wood through the winter.

Flowers: August–October
Height: 6–8ft (1.8–2.4m)
Pruning category: C

C. texensis 'Sir Trevor Lawrence'
Hybridizer: Jackman, 1890

This is the other surviving variety of Jackman's and was almost extinct until revived by Christopher Lloyd. I was able to obtain some propagating material from a plant in the possession of the late Sir William Lawrence, after whose grandfather, a former president of the Royal Horticultural Society, the plant was named. Since then, I have been responsible for distributing many hundreds of plants, and though still uncommon it is, at least, available again.

The flower is tulip-shaped like the other varieties, but it has a tendency to roll over at the tips. Common to all these hybrids is the brilliance of colour, a luminous crimson, shading to light violet around the edges in the case of 'Sir Trevor Lawrence'. There is not much colour on the outside, a creamy-green with reddish overtones; the stamens are cream.

Flowers: August–October
Height: 6–8ft (1.8–2.4m)
Pruning category: C

C. texensis 'The Princess of Wales'
Hybridizer: Fretwell, 1984

Although these brightly coloured hybrids seem to have almost universal appeal, none had been raised since the original crosses produced by the early pioneers. As the

Opposite: *C. texensis* 'Gravetye Beauty'

Opposite above: *C. texensis* 'Ladybird Johnson';   *C. texensis* 'The Princess of Wales'
opposite below: *C. texensis* 'Sir Trevor Lawrence'

majority of those have been lost to cultivation, it had always been my ambition to produce more of these gems of the clematis world. Not a speedy ambition to achieve, and the first of these hybrids to be created since the early 1900s took a period of eight years from start to sight of first flower. The culmination of this lengthy process was in being given the honour of naming it after H.R.H. The Princess of Wales. Two clematis had been named 'Princess of Wales' during the last century, but they appear to have died out before World War II. As they were large-flowered hybrids, there could be no confusion as to identity, even assuming a possible re-discovery.

Having the same trumpet-shape flowers as the previous hybrids, it has the added distinction of retaining this shape until sepal-fall. It is the most vividly coloured of any clematis hybrid yet raised; the deep, vibrant pink having a luminous quality to be seen rather than described. A further asset is that this deep pink extends to the outside of the sepals, further complemented by a prominent tuft of creamy-yellow stamens. The parentage was 'Bees Jubilee' × *C. texensis*.

Flowers: August–October
Height: 6–8ft (1.8–2.4m)
Pruning category: C

C. thibetana
Country of origin: Himalayas, Tibet, c.1885

An attractive, if not showy plant, which is distinguished by its ferny, glaucous foliage. Each leaf is usually divided into seven small leaflets, which are deeply cleft or irregularly lobed and have broad irregular teeth. They are as glaucous as any that I have come across among the orientalis types.

The flowers, which are not particularly eye-catching, are perhaps chiefly of interest to flower arrangers. They are about $1\frac{1}{2}$in (4–5cm) wide, broadly campanulate, the four pointed sepals slightly recurving at the tips and of a lime green-yellow colour. The filaments are muddy green with dull purple anthers. Vigorous, if not tall, *C. thibetana* needs a sunny position to flower well.

C. thibetana is sometimes sold under the name of *C. vernayi*.

Flowers: July–September
Height: 10ft (3m)
Pruning category: C

Opposite: *C. triternata* 'Rubro-marginata'

C. tosaensis
Country of origin: Japan

This closely resembles *C. japonica* except in colour. It bears hanging clusters of elongated, bell-shaped flowers, $1\frac{1}{4}$in (3cm) long, creamy-white and slightly downy on the outside, with crimped tips to the sepals; the stamens are cream. The ternate and serrated leaves are very similar to those of *C. japonica* but are a pale yellow-green.

Not an eye-catching species, it is pleasant enough and quite happy left to scramble over some low shrub.

Flowers: May–June
Height: 6–10ft (1.8–3m)
Pruning category: C

C. triternata 'Rubro-marginata'
Hybridizer: Jackman, 1863

This is sometimes incorrectly listed as *C. flammula* 'Rubro-marginata'. It is a hybrid of that species, with Jackman giving the other parent as *C. viticella* which appears to have donated mainly colouring to its offspring, as the general impression is that of flammula.

This easily-grown and trouble-free variety should be more widely appreciated, for it looks for all the world like a dusky-pink turbulent waterfall as it cascades down a small tree or tumbles over and along a sunny wall. Although the flowers, borne in large axillary and terminal panicles, have the same cruciform shape as flammula, individually they are larger, $1\frac{1}{2}$–2in (4–5 cm) across, purple-red shading to white towards the centre, with green stamens. They have the same hawthorn scent as flammula, although it is not as far reaching. The smooth-textured leaves are usually divided into five leaflets, each once or twice cleft or irregularly lobed.

Flowers: August–October
Height: 15–20ft (4.5–6m)
Pruning category: C

C. uncinata
Country of origin: China, 1848

Not all admirers of the glossy evergreen *C. armandii* have the large wall space necessary to accommodate that vigorous climber. This species is a far more tameable evergreen, rarely reaching more than 20ft (6m). Bean mentions some forms having five leaflets, but I have not met with this, and the plants that I received from China all have ternate leaves. The leaflets, 3–4in (8–10cm) long, are cordate, narrowly ovate tapering to points, dark green above with conspicuous veins and grey-green on the underside.

The stems are slender compared with *C. armandii* and distinctively ribbed. The white flowers are less striking, cruciform, 1½in (4cm) across, with large, conspicuous white stamens and they are borne in numerous panicles from the axils. The flowers are strongly scented. This species is less hardy than *C. armandii*.

Flowers: June–July
Height: 15ft (4.5m)
Pruning category: A

C. × vedrariensis and *C. × vedrariensis* 'Highdown'

Hybridizer: Vilmorin, 1914

This hybrid between *C. chrysocoma* and *C. montana* 'Rubens' combines the best of both parents. The flowers have the wide, rounded sepals of *C. chrysocoma*. The foliage, too, is wide and lobed like that species and has similarly golden hairs on the leaves and young shoots, less densely but profuse when compared with *C. spooneri*. The ternate leaves combine montana's serrated leaflets. The soft mauve-pink is deeper than *C. chrysocoma* and the flowers are produced, like those of montanas, in clusters from the axils of the previous year's growth.

C. × *vedrariensis* 'Highdown' was, reputedly, a vedrariensis seedling raised at that famous garden, and it is a far superior, deeper pink. It has the added advantage of a less exuberant habit than some of its relatives.

Flowers: May–June
Height: 20ft (6m)
Pruning category: A

C. versicolor

Country of origin: central USA, 1888

Truly a treasure of the clematis world and always a personal favourite, *C. versicolor* has neither large flowers, nor the bonus of scent or strong colours to attract, and yet it has that extra something that entices anyone to a closer inspection.

Closely related to *C. texensis*, it has the same urn-shaped, nodding flowers; they are smaller, ¾in (2cm) long, but more freely produced. The colour is strongest in the bud just before opening a strong purple-pink from the base to approximately halfway to the apex; in the expanded flower the colour fades to rosy-mauve pink. The pale cream colour of the tips is carried to the inside; the stamens are also pale cream. The leaves are also similar to those of texensis, having the same glaucous coloration with prominent, fine veining. There are normally six, widely ovate leaflets, the terminal one being replaced by a small tendril.

Exquisite scrambling over a small shrub, when the flowers drip from the branches like little jewels, in colder areas *C. versicolor* definitely requires the protection of a wall.

Flowers: July–September
Height: 5–7ft (1.5–2m)
Pruning category: C

C. verticillaris

Country of origin: eastern USA, 1797

This is the eastern cousin of *C. columbiana* (see page 98), with similarly wide-sepalled, rather droopy flowers. They have the same translucent quality with conspicuous veining, but the colour is mauve-pink or reddish-violet. The ternate leaves have the same smooth or occasionally toothed leaflets.

It has been my experience that this is easier to accommodate than *C. columbiana*, although it still represents a challenge to grow successfully.

Flowers: May
Height: 6–8ft (1.8–2.4m)
Pruning category: A

C. viorna

Country of origin: eastern USA, 1730

This species gave its name to a group of clematis with fleshy, urn-shaped flowers, found mainly in the USA. They are 1–1¼in (2.5–3cm) long, the four sharply-pointed sepals recurving at the tips. The usual colour is reddish-purple, shading to creamy-yellow towards the tips and inside; the stamens, too, are yellow. I have seen a most attractive form with sandy-orange flowers. As with all viornae types, the seed-heads are large and intriguing. The foliage consists of five to seven leaflets, ovate; the basal pair can be cleft, lobed or sometimes divided into two or three. In the wild, the species forms a woody framework; in Britain it usually dies back to ground level in winter.

Flowers: July–August
Height: 8ft (2.4m)
Pruning category: C

C. vitalba

Country of origin: Europe

It is ironic that Britain, a country where clematis from

Opposite above: *C. versicolor;* opposite below: *C. verticillaris*

C. viorna

all quarters of the world can be successfully grown, should have only one native species, and that one hardly exciting. It is the only hardy clematis capable of tackling a large forest tree such as a sycamore or beech and is best suited to a woodland garden.

The foliage of *C. vitalba* is large and coarse, the five leaflets up to 4in (10cm) long and coarsely serrated. Even though the flowers are borne profusely in large panicles, they are hardly likely to set the pulse racing. Individually they are about 1in (2.5cm) across, the four, narrow sepals downy and rolling back on to the stalk so that the stamens protrude like a bushy tuft. The colour is uninteresting, a dull creamy-white but the seed-heads are striking, the large, fluffy, silver-grey balls lasting well into the new year. *C. ligusticifolia* and *C. virginiana*, from the USA, are very closely related, less vigorous, but no more desirable.

Flowers: July–September
Height: 30–60ft (9–18m)
Pruning category: C

C. viticella
Country of origin: southern Europe, 1569

A garden-worthy plant in its own right, this species has made a valuable contribution to the production of the large-flowered hybrids. Still, in my opinion, it is the small-flowered hybrids derived from it that constitute one of the most important groups for garden decoration. Such a statement needs quantifying.

The majority of clematis sold are large-flowered hybrids, in their many-coloured varieties, and it is the lack of colour choice among the small viticella hybrids that is the main obstacle in the way of their wider appreciation. They are so prolific in bloom that having smaller flowers is no disadvantage as regards impact, especially as they give their all for a period of three months. An additional factor in their favour is their virtual freedom from wilt, the fungus disease that continues to bedevil their larger cousins and deters many people from trying these fine climbers.

C. viticella itself is variable as to quality of flower, some being very miserable things. In a good form, the four sepals would be widely ovate, tapering to points, in a nodding campanulate or saucer-shaped flower, $1\frac{1}{2}$–$2\frac{1}{2}$in (4–6cm) across, borne singly or in groups on a slender stalk. The colour would be a rich, deep purple, with small, green stamens; all too often the colouring is

Opposite above *C. vitalba*; opposite below: *C. viticella*

purple-grey. The leaves also vary, some having narrow leaflets, others quite rounded, but usually about 5in (13cm) long, divided into five or seven leaflets; some, not all, are further divided into three. A vigorous and easy plant, but the dark flowers need careful placing. The following hybrids offer a livelier selection.

Flowers: July–September
Height: 10–12ft (3–3.6m)
Pruning category: C

C. viticella 'Abundance'
Hybridizer: Morel, c.1900

Francisque Morel produced the majority of these hybrids. All have similarly shaped flowers to 'Abundance' unless described to the contrary. As with viticella, all flowers are produced on the last few feet of the current season's growth; slightly nodding, or held on the vertical plain, they are produced in solid sheets of bloom. 'Abundance' has flowers, 2–2½in (5–6cm) across, comprised of four or five widely obovate sepals with irregularly crimped edges, saucer-shaped but swept back towards the tips; a bright mauve-pink-red with deeper

C. viticella 'Abundance'

Opposite: *C. viticella* 'Alba Luxurians'

red veins. The stamens are creamy-green. One of the most striking hybrids in this group.

Flowers: July–September
Height: 10–12ft (3–3.6m)
Pruning category: C

C. viticella 'Alba Luxurians'
Hybridizer: Veitch, c.1900

When asked the impossible question, my wife invariably seeks refuge by mentioning this plant for its 'wayward fascination'. It certainly has the uncanny ability to enrapture almost everyone who sets eyes upon it.

The four or five sepalled flowers, 2½–3½in (6–8cm) long, are more narrowly campanulate than others in this group and of a more nodding habit. Opaque white, each sepal is tipped with bright green, and there is a telling eye of dark purple stamens. The first flowers of the season have sepals terminating in a green leaf-like extension, which some find intriguing. Either way, they soon settle down to their true livery.

Flowers: July–September
Height: 10–12ft (3–3.6m)
Pruning category: C

C. viticella 'Elvan'

Hybridizer: Fretwell, 1979

The 2in (5cm) flowers have four, slightly twisted sepals in a soft, warm purple, with feathered creamy-white central stripes. It has a more nodding habit, after the manner of viticella, and is one of the more vigorous in this group.

Flowers: July–September
Height: 10–12ft (3–3.6m)
Pruning category: C

C. viticella 'Etoile Violette'

Hybridizer: Morel, 1885

One of the most free-flowering of any hybrid, the flowers are so abundantly produced that they pile one on the other, almost obscuring the foliage. They are larger than those of 'Abundance', 3–4in (8–10cm) across, the four, five or, usually, six sepals giving a more rounded outline. The deep purple colour is rather flat, but is lifted by the prominent tuft of creamy-yellow stamens.

Flowers: July–September
Height: 10–12ft (3–3.6m)
Pruning category: C

C. viticella 'Little Nell'

Hybridizer: Morel, c.1900

Masses of 2in (5cm) flowers, with slightly more narrow, pointed sepals usually six in number. White, with broad, peripheral, pale pink bands and green stamens. The leaves are pinnate as in viticella, but the leaflets are larger and more rounded.

Flowers: July–September
Height: 10–12ft (3–3.6m)
Pruning category: C

C. viticella 'Margot Koster'

Hybridizer: Morel

Included in this composite group are a few varieties with larger flowers than the majority. They are occasionally listed among the large-flowered hybrids in some literature and catalogues. When a large-flowered hybrid is crossed with C. viticella, the resultant seedlings will show not only flowers 5–6in (13–15cm) in size with the characteristics of both parents, but also small-flowered varieties very reminiscent of viticella. If the

Opposite: *C. viticella* 'Etoile Violette'

closest affinity of the new plant is to viticella – slightly larger flowers notwithstanding – it is more sensible to include it here.

'Margot Koster' has gappy flowers, 4in (10cm) across, with four, five or six long obovate sepals, curled and reflexed in a rather informal way. Individually the flowers are uninspiring, but this variety has the similar attribute of 'Etoile Violette', sheeting a solid wall of flower. The colour, a deep rosy-pink, looks more effective from a distance. The five leaflets are longer and more rounded.

Flowers: July–September
Height: 10–12ft (3–3.6m)
Pruning category: C

C. viticella 'Mary Rose'

'Mary Rose' came my way in 1981 through the observation of a customer. She had admired a plant growing at the entrance to a friend's home and queried whether it was in general commerce. I was subsequently invited to view the plant, growing on the wall of a mansion in the southwest of England, its multiple stems looking akin to a tree trunk.

The flower was fully double, resembling C. viticella 'Purpurea Plena Elegans', but was smaller and spiky. I saw it as it needs to be seen: in full sun, doing justice to its smoky-amethyst colouring. Research verified that this plant could not be attributed to Morel as it pre-dates his work. A very good illustration of it is on the plate titled 'August' in Robert Furber's *Twelve Months of Flowers* (1730). Parkinson, in 1629, described this double 'of a dull or sad blewish purple colour which produced no seed', making this the oldest clematis cultivar known. We felt that a more generally acceptable name was needed than the previous 'double purple Virgin's Bower'. The parallels of its beginning and resurgence with Henry VIII's flagship settled its new name. The foliage is identical to that of viticella, and it is an exceptionally vigorous and free-flowering plant, the sterile flowers extending an already long season.

Flowers: July–September
Height: 10–12ft (3–3.6m)
Pruning category: C

C. viticella 'Mme Julia Correvon'

Hybridizer: Morel, 1900

This, like 'Margot Koster', has large flowers, 4in (10cm) across, although appearing smaller. The four, five or normally six sepals are narrower and taper to points, undulating and reflexed. Its colouring is one of the best in the red shades, the bright, clear rosy-red keeping its colour through to sepal-fall. The yellow stamens

C. viticella 'Mary Rose'

contrast well, being larger than is normal for this group. The foliage is as viticella but with larger leaflets. A very good performer over a generously long flowering season.

Flowers: July–September
Height: 10–12ft (3–3.6m)
Pruning category: C

C. viticella 'Minuet'
Hybridizer: Morel

Very similar to viticella, with four, sometimes five, sepals, the flowers are 2in (5cm) across. The ground colour is off-white, shading to a rose-purple peripheral band; the stamens are green. The foliage is as 'Little Nell' (see page 149).

Flowers: July–September
Height: 10–12ft (3–3.6m)
Pruning category: C

C. viticella 'Purpurea Plena Elegans'

Almost from the time of its introduction, *C. viticella* has shown a predilection for producing double-flowered 'sports' (see, for instance, 'Mary Rose', page 149). They were presumably seedling 'sports', as sterile forms usually are.

Quite a number of people find no attraction in double flowers. However, some who dislike this feature in the large-flowered clematis still find fascination in the small, multi-sepalled rosettes. They measure 2–2½in (5–6cm) across, with the mass of narrow sepals recurved in the manner of a reflex chrysanthemum. Soft rosy-purple in colour, lavender-grey on the reverse and, as is usual with sterile flowers, they last for ages. It is as vigorous and free-flowering as the type.

Flowers: July–September
Height: 10–12ft (3–3.6m)
Pruning category: C

Opposite above: *C. viticella* 'Mme Julia Correvon'; opposite below: *C. viticella* 'Purpurea Plena Elegans'

C. viticella 'Royal Velours'
Hybridizer: Morel

A well-named plant with a sheen that leads one to expect the texture of velvet, so deeply rich that imaginative interplanting is called for, such as the sharp orange of *Eccremocarpus scaber*. As in the nature of other viticella hybrids, it flings itself 10–12ft (3–3.6m) in all directions and flowers with equal abandon.

Leaves, 4–5in (10–12cm) long, are divided into three to five leaflets; each leaflet is further divided into three to five segments, more rounded than viticella. The four, blunt-edged, overlapping sepals form a saucer-shaped flower 2½in (6cm) across; opening a rich reddish-purple, it fades to purple. The anthers are reddish-purple, the filaments shading to green.

Flowers: July–September
Height: 10–12ft (3–3.6m)
Pruning category: C

C. viticella 'Rubra'
Hybridizer: unknown

An old variety that, although confused with, and sold

C. viticella 'Tango'

under the name of, the now defunct 'Kermesina', has always concurred with the same description. The flowers, 2in (5cm) across, have four or five widely obovate sepals with a textured surface; they are bright crimson with a white spot at the base of each. The stamens are muddy green, and the styles are almost black.

Flowers: July–September
Height: 10–12ft (3–3.6m)
Pruning category: C

C. viticella 'Tango'
Hybridizer: Fretwell, 1986

A jolly little flower, 2in (5cm) wide, the four or five sepals are white, with a bright crimson network of fine veins and a broad band around the edges. The stamens have green filaments and brown anthers. There are masses of flowers, and it is a vigorous grower.

Flowers: July–September
Height: 10–12ft (3–3.6m)
Pruning category: C

Opposite above: *C. viticella* 'Royal Velours'; opposite below: *C. viticella* 'Rubra'

153

Opposite: *C. viticella* 'Venosa Violacea'

C. viticella 'Venosa Violacea'

Hybridizer: Lemoine, c.1910

Although the flowers are large for this group, and it sits none too comfortably with the remainder of its companions, it is too distinguished a plant to place among the homogenous hybrids. *C. viticella* is not in doubt as one parent; it is the characteristics that point to the other that are intriguing.

The five or six sepals form a flower 4in (10cm) across, each sepal recurved along its length. The white ground colour has overlying veins in purple, increasing in density towards the edges; along the centre the veins are more red, especially towards the tips. The filaments are green, shading purple to the blackish-purple anthers; the styles, too, form a dark eye. Halfway along the flower stalk are a pair of bracts as in *C. florida*. The leaves are large and ternate or sometimes there are five leaflets, again subdivided into three, some lobed, and with little resemblance to those of viticella.

Although *C. florida* has always been quoted as one of the parents of many of the large-flowered hybrids, there is no reference to it by any of the early hybridizers. When one looks at 'Venosa Violacea', the foliage and particularly the bracts and stamens, they bear so close a resemblance to *C. florida* that this is most probably the other parent and possibly 'Venosa Violacea' the only hybrid from it.

It does not have the vigour of viticella nor the mass flowering, but it is nevertheless an easy-going plant, flowering over a long season, and so distinctive that it cannot be confused with any other.

Flowers: June–September
Height: 8–10ft (2.4–3m)
Pruning category: C

Clematis patens

GLOSSARY

Anther The pollen-bearing tip of the stamen.

Axil The junction between leaf and stem.

Bipinnate Twice pinnate.

Biternate Ternate leaflets again divided into three.

Bract A leaf-like structure on the flower stem.

Campanulate Bell-shaped.

Cordate Heart-shaped.

Cuspidate Abruptly and sharply pointed.

Dioecious Male and female flowers are borne on separate plants.

Filament The stalk of the stamen.

Glaucous Bluish or bluish-grey

Hermaphrodite Male and female organs within the same flower.

Lanceolate Wide above the base, tapering narrowly to the point.

Monoecious Male and female flowers are separate, but borne on the same plant.

Node The point at which leaves are attached to the stem.

Obovate Widest above the middle of a leaf or sepal.

Ovate Widest below the middle of a leaf or sepal.

Pinnate More than three leaflets arranged either side of a central stalk.

Sepal A modified leaf, in clematis taking the place of a petal.

Serrated Having saw-like teeth.

Stamen The male organ of a flower, combining the filament and anther.

Staminode A sterile stamen, often petal-like.

Ternate Divided into three parts.

× The hybridization sign.

INDEX